100

TREEN
or Small Woodware

1   A Welsh turner using a pole-lathe

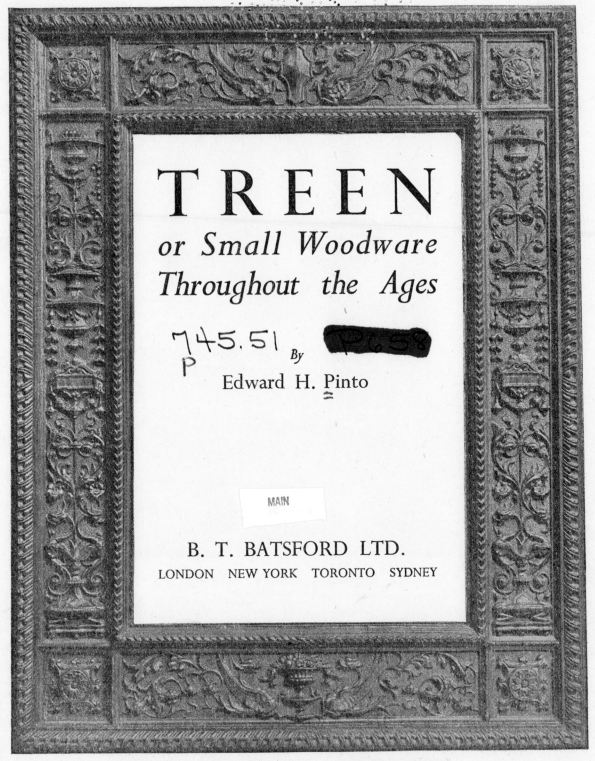

TREEN

or Small Woodware Throughout the Ages

By

Edward H. Pinto

B. T. BATSFORD LTD.

LONDON   NEW YORK   TORONTO   SYDNEY

DEDICATION

To my wife, who for many months has taken notes, listed, typed, telephoned, investigated, corrected, pursued, purchased, polished, de-wormed, and tumbled over treen.

First Published, 1949

Printed in Great Britain by
SPOTTISWOODE, BALLANTYNE & CO. LTD., LONDON & COLCHESTER
for the Publishers, B. T. BATSFORD, LTD., LONDON : 15 North Audley Street, W.1
and Malvern Wells, Worcestershire

NEW YORK: 122, East 55th Street.   TORONTO : 480–6, University Avenue
SYDNEY : 156 Castlereagh Street

ACKNOWLEDGMENT

The absence of a bibliography is regretted; lack of any comprehensive books on treen is the reason. "Domestic Utensils of Wood" by the late Owen Evan-Thomas is the only book which I know devoted entirely to treen. It has been impossible to avoid quoting a few references that Mr. Evan-Thomas used, but nearly all the text is the result of fresh research and the majority of objects illustrated have never been previously photographed.

Most of the written information available regarding treen has, until now, occurred in scattered references in old books, mainly on other subjects, in guides to collections, or in short articles which have appeared in historical and art journals. The investigation necessary to bring to light and collate the data for writing this book has had to be largely of a pioneer nature, drawn from varied sources and many people. It has entailed considerable travel, has led to meetings with many charming and helpful people and the forming of new friendships. In fact, the writing of the book has given as much pleasure as the collecting of those items of my wife's and my treen with which it is illustrated.

The Author and Publishers wish to thank the following authorities and individuals for permission to reproduce examples from their collections: Mr. R. J. A. Arundell, Wardour Castle, for Figs. 12 and 13; Mr. H. Baer, Davies St., London, for Fig. 68; Mr. T. W. Bagshawe, F.S.A., F.R.Hist.S., and Mrs. Bagshawe, Cambridge, for Fig. 93; British Museum, for Figs. 15, 16 and 17; Mr. Moir Carnegie, F.S.A., for Fig. 20; Colchester Museum, for Fig. 116; Dansk Folkemuseum, Copenhagen, for Fig. 125; Messrs. Emil, Burlington Gardens, for Fig. 103; Glasgow Art Gallery and Museum and Sir William Burrell, for Figs. 21, 22 and 24; Haslemere Museum and Messrs. Dryad, Ltd., for Figs. 128 and 131; Commander G. E. R. How, R.N., Sloane St., London, for Figs. 18 and 25; Mr. Courtenay Ilbert, Milner St., London, for Figs. 94 and 95; Messrs. H. M. Lee & Sons, Ripley, Surrey, for Fig. 23; National Museum of Antiquities of Scotland, for Fig. 28; National Museum of Dublin, for Fig. 31; National Museum of Wales, for Figs. 1, 11, 40, 41, 53 and 66; Royal Botanic Gardens, Kew, for Figs. 104 and 114; Rev. C. J. Sharp, Shepreth, Herts., for Figs. 10, 35, 38, 39, 42, 49, 52, 69, 75, 85, 91 and 118; Taunton Castle Museum, for Fig. 27; Victoria and Albert Museum, for Figs. 5, 19, 45, 71, 83, 96, 111, 112 and 127. The remainder of the illustrations are selected from our collection of between two and three thousand pieces of treen. For the patience and skill in photographing them, my thanks are due to Mr. Sydney Newbery, F.I.B.P., F.R.P.S.

The following have been good enough to provide me with generous information from their store of knowledge:

Commander G. E. R. How, R.N. (The Tulloch Mazer and McIntosh coconut cup); Mr. W. A. Thorpe and Mr. C. C. Oman, of The Victoria and Albert Museum (General and historical); Mr. A. B. Tonnochy, M.A., F.S.A., of the British Museum (General and historical); The Norsk Folkemuseum, Oslo (General and historical); The Nordiska Museum, Stockholm (General and historical); The Rev. C. J. Sharp, Shepreth, Herts (General and historical); Mr. H. St. George Gray, M.A., F.S.A., of Taunton Castle Museum (The Whistling Cup); Mr. R. J. A. Arundell, of Wardour Castle (The Glastonbury Tankard); Miss C. Baker, M.A., of Bucks County Museum, Aylesbury (General and historical); Miss A. M. Buck, B.A., of Luton Public Museum (identification and history of lace bobbins); Mr. W. T. O'Dea, B.Sc., A.M.I.E.E., of the Science Museum, and the Directors of Messrs. Bryant & May (Fire making and lighting); The Directors of Messrs. Fords Blotting Paper (Blotting paper); Mr. H. Baer, Davies Street, London (General and historical); Dr. Joseph Raftery, of the National Museum, Dublin (Historical and general information on Irish drinking vessels); Mr. Iorwerth C. Peate, M.A., F.S.A., and Mr. Ffransis Payne of the National Museum of Wales, Cardiff (A wealth of information regarding folk life and customs in Wales); Mr. Courtenay Ilbert (Watches); Mr. Roland Champness, M.A., LL.M., of the Worshipful Company of Turners (Turnery); Commander H. B. Tuffill, C.B.E., R.D., R.N.R., and the Master and Wardens of the Worshipful Company of Vintners (English drinking vessels); Mr. D. H. Woolley of Mount Street, London (Wine measures) ; Mr. J. Hutchinson, LL.D., F.R.S., Mr. F. N. Howes, D.Sc., and Mr. C. R. Metcalfe, M.A., Ph.D., of the Royal Botanic Gardens, Kew (Historical information and identification of wood and nuts); Mr. G. F. Skinner, B.Sc., of the Science Museum (for placing at my disposal the records of the Museum appertaining to weights and measures and for much instructive data); Dr. W. O'Sullivan of the National Museum, Dublin, Mr. G. T. Stoodley, Chief Inspector, Weights and Measures Department, Corporation of London, Mr. T. G. Poppy, Standards Department, Board of Trade, London, Mr. J. Thomasson, Chief Inspector, Weights and Measures, Preston, Lancs, and Messrs. W. & T. Avery Ltd., Birmingham (Weights and measures); Miss E. Gerrard, A.L.A., Worthing Museum and Art Gallery (General and historical); Mr. T. Thornton Wills, of Messrs. W. D. & H. O. Wills, Bristol (Pipes); Mr. Ian Finlay, Royal Scottish Museum, Edinburgh, Mr. Andrew Hannah, M.A., Dip.A., Glasgow Art Gallery and Museums, Mr. B. K. Stevenson, M.A., National Museum of Antiquities of Scotland, and Miss I. F. Grant, Am Gasgadh, Kingussie (Historical and general information on Scottish drinking vessels) ; the late Sir Geoffrey Callender, M.A., F.S.A., of the National Maritime Museum, Greenwich, Sir Alan Moore, of Battle, Sussex, Captain F. C. P. Naish, of Old Bursledon, Hants, and Mr. J. D. White, LL.D., of Burton Court, Chelsea (Sailmakers' tools); Mr. B. R. S. Megaw, B.A., F.S.A., of the Manx Museum, Douglas, I.O.M. (General and historical); Mr. W. A. Whittle, of Hall-i'-th'-Wood Folk Museum (General and historical); Mr. J. F. Parker, F.S.A., and Mrs. Parker of Tickenhill Manor Private Folk Museum, Bewdley (General and historical); Mr. D. W. Herdman of Cheltenham Museum (Gambrels); Mr. J. A. Stendall, M.R.I.A., of the Museum and Art Gallery, Belfast (General and historical).

Finally, my thanks are due in an especial degree to Mr. Thomas W. Bagshawe, F.S.A., F.R.Hist.S., of the Luton Museum, for providing a veritable fountain of direct information and constructive criticism, as well as acting as general guide to various other sources of knowledge.

E. H. PINTO

LONDON—*December, 1948*

CONTENTS

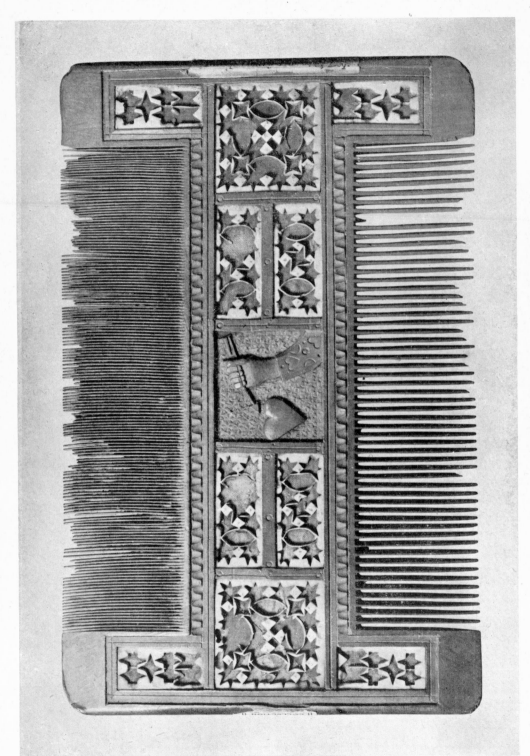

2 Fine quality mediæval comb carved from a single piece of boxwood and inlaid with fretted bone ornament

3 Some miscellanea of the dining table, including an early trencher with salt cavity. Bottom right, alternative centres for table combination in 8

4 18th century garnishing skewers, various nutcrackers, some platters, dish slopes, knife rests and egg cups

INTRODUCTION

The *Oxford Dictionary* defines "treen" as "(i) made of tree; wooden (ii) of or belonging to, obtained or made from a tree or trees—1670". This definition is sufficiently broad to cover furniture, joinery, old-time ships, road vehicles and many things not generally included in this term.

References to treen are numerous in old English literature, particularly to chalices, cups, bowls, platters and "services of treen". Never, I think, has the term been applied to any object larger than, say, a spinning wheel. Moreover, it is not generally interpreted as covering objects designed primarily for ornament, such as carved figures.

In other words, the term "treen" usually described the miscellanea of small wooden objects in daily domestic or farm use and in trades and professions, and only objects within this scope are included in this book.

Even so, the wealth of objects is so vast that I have had to restrict the data and illustrations primarily to work of European turners, coopers, general woodworkers and handymen and exclude most objects made by cabinetmakers. The chief exception is the inclusion of particular objects which were sometimes made in the form of turnery and at others as cabinet craft, or where they were formed by a combination of the two trades. The Tunbridge wares, a notable range of articles coming under these headings but not included in this book, will be the subject of another book.

Whilst fitness for purpose was originally the first qualification of treen, beauty of form and love of craftsmanship were rarely overlooked and great care was taken in selecting suitable timber to provide desired shape, colour, grain and ornament. Probably treen is so satisfying because it is mostly peasant art and that being a natural or unconscious form of expression, becomes ornamented construction, not constructed ornament, as is so much of the self-conscious "arty" art of to-day. There are few lapses into positive bad taste until the nineteenth century and even then treen was among the lesser offenders. Many treen objects are amusing because of crudity of form or ornament and comparatively few British examples are made by great artists, who usually preferred working precious metals. In Italy, where close grained hardwoods, such as box, were more readily obtainable, some great artists did make treen and a few examples of their superb craftsmanship are illustrated.

Occasionally, in a particular example, fitness for purpose is submerged in the desire to create an intricate or artistic masterpiece, but such cases are comparatively rare; examples illustrated are the "Shakespeare" pipe stopper (60) and the elaborate knitting sheath (77), neither of which were probably intended to have or have had use.

Love tokens too, though originally they mostly started as useful objects, such as spoons, lace bobbins, stay busks, or knitting sheaths, sometimes just crudely carved with the donor's and recipient's names or initials and an arrow-pierced heart or other device, often developed into mere wooden "Valentines". This applies particularly to love spoons (40), (41) and (42). All these love tokens, however, are so much part of the folk-lore and peasant history of these islands and possess so much simple charm and interest, that the custom which they commemorate itself justifies recording them as useful wooden objects. All the love, devotion and desire to please and excel, which the donor could not express in words, are carved in these wood symbols. The hours of joyous and creative thought and labour had no commercial and little practical motive and they represent, therefore, in some ways the purest expression of peasant art—simple gifts which money could not buy. That these tokens were indeed

B

labours of love is obvious when we consider the effort needed to execute them, often after a twelve-hour working day, by candle or rush light, with a pocket knife as the only tool available to a modest purse.

Amongst the treen illustrated are a few bone, ivory and horn objects. These are included because they were made and decorated by the same artisans, for the same purposes as their wood counterparts and they provide interesting comparisons.

Until the mid-seventeenth century, the history of treen is mostly the history of turning and consists of objects or parts of objects, such as a bowl and cover, each sufficiently small to be made from a single piece of wood. Where it was necessary to join two parts of an article to form the whole, turnery again was the junction usually employed as either threaded pin and socket, or as two engaging threaded rims. The period from the fall of Rome to the sixteenth century was the age of dry construction and where treen was required in frame or box form, it had to follow the dry draw-peg method of jointing used in joinery and furniture at that time. This is shown in the English tilting hob (34). Alternative methods of dry box-construction are discussed in Part 16—"Treen of North-West Europe".

From the seventeenth century onwards, the cabinet designer and cabinetmaker came increasingly into the field of treen, partially as the result of changing conditions of living and specialised needs resulting from a higher standard of comfort and partially due to the rediscovery of glue for constructional purposes. Highly moisture resistent adhesives only reached the commercial stage about 1930, so although the non-moisture resisting animal glue in use before then did not affect the design of treen which was subject to wetting, it did bring in the cabinetmaker for such new specialities as fitted boxes for writing, dressing and needlework and for tea caddies, wine coolers, etc., which were often superb pieces made *en suite* with fashionable furniture of the day. It is hoped to include these and the like in another book.

This book, whilst illustrating some outstandingly rare or fine specimens, concentrates mainly on everyday treen used by "Everyman" and his wife and the illustrations have been chosen to indicate the almost unlimited range, both in variety and size, which exists and how treen collecting can be fascinating for the man of small means or of long purse. Although I have in my collection over two thousand pieces, it does not include even one example of many objects. As a particular object was often made in hundreds or thousands of designs, sizes and varieties of wood, how enormous must have been the range.

Very rarely is treen found surviving from earlier than the sixteenth century and most is eighteenth century or later although, judging from literature, eating, drinking and cooking treen was losing ground in the seventeenth century to pewter, copper and earthenware. That so much more eighteenth- and nineteenth-century treen has survived is due to the shorter period since its creation and to the fact that although the percentage of treen-using population was decreasing, the total population of the British Isles rose from about 4¾ millions in 1600 A.D. to 6 millions in 1700 and to over 16 millions in 1800. The reason for this last sharp increase is discussed in Part 5.

Whilst the care taken to preserve some vessels of rare wood, fine workmanship or exceptional size is understandable, it is surprising that so much simple treen has survived, particularly considering its almost complete lack of value and the small labour of replacing it when worn. Nevertheless, much has been preserved with almost sentimental care. Typical is the wooden platter (3), which has been copper riveted and patched.

An amusement which occurs in collecting treen is in trying to identify the purpose of an article. Wood being such an easy and friendly material and one requiring few tools

5   A fine set of Elizabethan roundels, with original case

6 Mainly 18th century salts and condiment pots

7 Some of the infinite variety of treen nutcrackers

and little training for simple work, it is not unusual to find a piece created by a man to meet his particular need and where no counterpart or written description exists, only a hazard can be made as to original purpose. Such a case is the small, thin, curiously shaped boxwood panel (left, 115). For years its purpose eluded me until a visitor gave what I think is the correct solution, which will be found in Part 14. I still possess, however, a few mystery pieces. Another complication is that treen, when found, is often wrongly described, altered or incomplete. The strainer bowl (36) was labelled in a shop window "nice bowl for bulbs"! The cheese moulds (51) had all been "improved" by having their "weep" holes filled with plastic wood! The rare silk thrower (72) had an even more remarkable adventure: its lower half was bought in an auction "lot" described as a knitting sheath and some months later I found the other half in an antique dealer's shop.

Although the word "treen" has great antiquity, treen itself need not be old and as the small useful woodware of to-day is the treen of to-morrow, a few modern objects are illustrated. Hogarth was right in being enraged at the fashionable men of his day, who neglected great living artists and valued pictures for their antiquity. He neatly made his point in a painting exhibited at the Society of Artists in 1761, in which he depicted a foppishly dressed ape assiduously watering three dead plants.

The turnery side of treen-making is much more alive than most people realise. The 1936 Forestry Commission report on "The Demand for Timber in Wood-turning in Great Britain" stated that at that time there were 60,000 people engaged in the industry. Admittedly much turnery now being made is not "treen", but parts of larger objects. Nevertheless, there is a thriving trade in reels, shuttles and bobbins for the textile trades, brush parts, lasts, indoor and outdoor tool handles, mallets, dowels, sports goods, gun stocks, door knobs, toys, washing dollies and clothes pegs, kitchen and dairy utensils, tableware, patterns, umbrella parts and walking sticks, knitting needles, buttons, etc. Beech remains the turner's most popular wood, with sycamore second, birch third, oak and ash a joint fourth and elm next. Other home grown woods used include alder, lime, walnut, horse and sweet chestnut, poplar, hazel, hornbeam, apple, pear and yew. Of the imported timbers, the favourites are various species of pine, mahogany, lignum vitæ, box, maple, hickory, ebony, persimmon and teak.

An ever increasing percentage of modern turnery is executed on automatic lathes which, without operational skill, produce thousands of repetition articles identical in size and form. Before automatic lathes were introduced, no branch of wood machining required as much operational skill as turnery. It is not generally realised that the old machine did not do the work, in the sense that other machines do. All it did was firmly hold and revolve a piece of wood between two points, so that the turner with his true eye, his skill and his steady hand on chisel could make it take the desired form and dimension. As even the most skilled turner does not turn two articles precisely alike unless he tests with jigs and callipers, and as testing to such fine limits wastes needless time for articles of general utility, much of the charm of ancient pieces lies in their slight variations of curves and dimensions. Although not really treen, balusters are a good example of this theory: the balusters of a sixteenth- or seventeenth-century staircase never give any sense of monotony, even if they be all of the same design because there are considerable variations between each. Such variations do not occur in the best designed modern work and, consequently, repetition now tends to monotony.

From prehistoric times until the advent of the automatic lathe, each improvement in the machine was concentrated on saving manual labour, not human skill, which remained paramount.

The pole-lathe, which was the earliest, has a reciprocal motion, not a rotatory one as have lathes operated by hand wheel, foot treadle and power which, in this sequence, were the later improvements. Nevertheless all these types are still used to-day. In PLATE 1, photographed in 1905, James Davies of Abercych, Pembrokeshire, is turning a bowl on a pole-lathe.

An excellent description of this work is given by Dr. Iorwerth C. Peate, M.A., F.S.A., in *Guide to the Collection Illustrating Welsh Folk Crafts and Industries*, obtainable from the National Museum of Wales, Cardiff.

In describing the tools used by the turners, Dr. Peate says:

> "The tools used by these turners are simple hook tools, which are made by the turners themselves, the correct tempering of the metal being considered a fine art. The cutting-end of each tool is curved round into a semi-circle, the one tool being used for the hollowing of the vessel turned, and the other for the shaping of the outside of the vessel. With continuous motion in the work, as in the ordinary lathe, the tendency is for the tool to become fixed or clogged by the accumulation of shavings, so rendering the tools unmanageable. In this respect, therefore, the intermittent motion of the pole-lathe is valuable, since the tools cut on the down stroke only; the up stroke, being against the tool, clears away the shavings. The Pembrokeshire turners assert, too, that the adjustability of the pole-lathe rest gives such an angle that the tool can be worked 'with the grain' and so prevent the scraping of the surfaces of the turned vessel. On the other hand, the working of the pole-lathe is much more laborious than that of an ordinary lathe, and when the vessel turned is of large dimensions, the energy required for working the treadle and manipulating the tool is such that one turner assured the writer that ten years at a pole-lathe would have made him 'a broken man'."

Some of the treen of yesterday, like the old type lathes, still remains in use: not all has qualified for the museum; much still serves its original purpose and many other pieces can be adapted to modern needs without spoiling them as specimens. Turned bowls, cheese moulds, measures, mortars, drinking vessels, spill vases, etc., some just as they are, others with metal liners, make ideal flower vases and jardinières, their simplicity setting off the flowers to full advantage. They also have the advantage of being almost indestructible, whilst requiring minimum cleaning. Wall knife boxes, salt boxes and candle boxes are useful in the hall for hat and clothes brushes, dog leads, torches, etc. Wine coolers and large flour barrels make attractive and serviceable waste paper receptacles and many other pleasant adaptations are practical.

Photographs of groups of different articles give a good idea of size by comparison with each other, but illustrations of single pieces convey no idea of size, so where sole objects of rarity or unusual size are shown, dimensions are given in the text.

It is regrettable that England possesses no National Museum of Peasant Art, although in several small collections treen can be examined against the appropriate backgrounds. Many of our large museums have fine collections of treen scattered among other exhibits but few collect their treen together or place it in suitable settings. Wales has set a good example: the National Museum at Cardiff has incomparably the best displayed collection of peasant art in the British Isles, as well as some excellent peasant rooms, suitably furnished and with their correct treen. Not satisfied with this beginning, Wales is planning an open air folk museum on the lines of those in Scandinavia and in Holland. The Earl of Plymouth has given St. Fagan's Castle and 18 acres for a folk museum and has arranged to transfer, on very favourable terms, a further 80 acres of St. Fagan's Park for development as a cultural and historical centre. As circumstances enjoin and funds permit, suitable houses of various dates and character, water mills, smithies, turners' shops and farms will be rebuilt on the site and fitted with their correct furniture and furnishings: old type wagons, harrows and other agricultural appliances will be housed in the sheds and looms and other devices in the mills, until the whole will represent a complete cross section of Welsh life before the Industrial Revolution.

Some disappointment may be felt that so many of the objects illustrated are only dated very approximately and that their wood is not mentioned in some cases. Regarding the date, the difficulties are that the same forms for the simpler objects continued from generation to generation in the country; city fashions largely by-passed or only reached them after considerable time lags. No design books or great names guide in treen as in furniture and there are few dated pieces. Our meagre knowledge consists of a few dated pieces, mostly drinking vessels, love tokens and documentary records and a few pictures, which occasionally show a piece of treen in their composition. The dates when various foreign woods were first imported and the resemblance of various treen objects to counterparts in glass, silver, pewter, etc., also form guides. The last can be misleading because sometimes treen was the contemporary of other materials—as occurred in standing cups, which both in treen and in silver had their heyday in the first quarter of the seventeenth century—in other cases, metal and glass slavishly followed the designs of treen, while sometimes country pieces, after varying time lags, followed the designs of city silver or glass.

Trying to identify the wood of a particular piece of treen is often worse than trying to settle the date; in fact, it is sometimes impossible without destroying the specimen. Experience of wood and woodworking count enormously, but the real expert hesitates to commit himself after a quick glance, knowing that there are some 30,000 identified varieties of hardwoods as well as 75 varieties of softwoods. He may hazard an opinion and, if he does, it is usually correct, but he knows that identification of wood by long grain, figure, colour and weight is at best equivalent to facial identification of humans, open to grave error by the inexpert. There is only one way of identifying wood with any certainty and that, the equivalent of finger prints, is by microscopic examination of a carefully prepared section of end grain. Colour, long grain and weight help, but can be very misleading even in large pieces of furniture while to be dogmatic about small pieces of wood, discoloured by fats, wines or other stains, faded or darkened by age and often carved over the whole of their surface and then varnished, is a case of fools stepping in where angels fear to tread.

A number of my pieces were formerly in another collection in which many were labelled not wisely but too well. The only thing which can be stated is that many of the labels are wrong but, for the reasons already given, it is quite impractical, in most instances, to say what would be right. In one particularly flagrant example, horn is described as sycamore. In doubtful cases undoubtedly the best policy is silence and that is the reason for so many "wooden" silences in this book. From most of the objects illustrated, it was not feasible to remove slices of end grain for identification, so often where I have named a wood, the naming is based merely on experience and the word "probably" should, in fact, be inserted before the name.

In spite of these shortcomings, I hope that this book, telling something of the history, customs and habits of our ancestors in Europe generally and in these islands particularly, will stimulate interest and inspire further research among collectors and all who love treen and the past.

The photographs may also help those who are striving to improve industrial design of the future and are not too proud to seek inspiration from the best and warning from the worst woodware of the past.

The collectors notes at the end of each chapter should prove useful in enabling collectors to compare their own specimens with those in museums and in assisting recognition of features, forms and age of treen. I have only mentioned specimens in those museums which I have visited or of which I have received comprehensive details. I confess my feeling of guilt at omission of mention of many fine collections, of which I am ignorant and also of those known to me, which I have not yet had time to view.

18　The Tulloch Mazer.　A magnificent Scottish specimen, dated 1557

19 A 17th century silver mounted pearwood standing cup with a nest of five "tumblers."

20 Three 17th century standing wassail bowls, two of lignum vitæ, one of yew wood

was used commonly, but meant an iron-hooped wooden tub for carrying water. It was employed in this sense until about A.D. 1600, although slightly before then it was also applied to large drinking vessels. Men who carried water from the London conduits are referred to in old records as "tankard bearers" and their vessels as tankards. References occur to tankards of this type in thirteenth- and fourteenth-century farming accounts and kitchen inventories.

Early drinking tankards were staved and bound by wattle hoops. They had wooden lids and handles, were lined with pitch and held two quarts. Hoping to decrease drunkenness, King Edgar introduced peg or pin tankards. He ordered cups with pins or nails inserted and ordained that he who drank past the mark at one draught should forfeit a penny, half to go to the accuser and half to the town where the offence occurred. This is an early instance of encouraging the common informer. Tankards were usually passed from hand to hand, the contents being divided by pegs into eight portions. The idea apparently proved abortive, for soon Archbishop Anselm decreed that "priests shall not drink to pins". Tankards, however, have retained their popularity and the phrase "Have a peg" has become common usage.

Most lidded wooden tankards surviving are Scandinavian (134) and date from the seventeenth to nineteenth century, but one genuine Saxon peg tankard survives. It is the "Glastonbury Tankard" (12 and 13), belonging to the family of Arundell of Wardour, Tisbury, Wiltshire. It is heavily lacquered and to this fact and the care with which it was secreted at moments of peril, we owe its remarkable state of preservation.

The lid is framed in a boldly carved border and the circular centre panel is carved with a scene of the Crucifixion, with the Virgin, St. John and winged angel heads to right and left of the Cross. A carved bunch of grapes forms the thumb lever for lifting the lid. Around the upper part of the body, below a rope moulding, are carved and labelled reliefs of the twelve Apostles, each in an arch. Below them are alternate carved flowers and swans. Round the base are pairs of grinning serpents; lions couchant form the three feet; the handle is gracefully scrolled.

The tankard belonged originally to Glastonbury Abbey and is said to have been blessed at the high table in the refectory; by the time of the suppression of the monastries, it was regarded with sufficient veneration to be handed to a dumb monk for delivery to a Roman Catholic layman for safety.

Sometime before the Civil War, it came into the possession of the Lords Arundell of Wardour and when Blanche, Lady Arundell, the second Baron's wife, eventually had to surrender her castle to Parliamentary troops, she saved the precious relic by secreting it on her person, a feat impossible to a lady in modern attire.

Tankards, and ladles also, are sometimes found with whistles in the handles, so that "you could whistle for it" when desiring a refill. Most writers claim that this originated the phrase "wet your whistle", but some contend that the phrase goes back further and that "whistle" in this sense is a corruption of "weasand" the windpipe, in former days sometimes spelt "weesil" or "wizzel".

MAZERS—Owing to their eleborate silver mounts, mazers are usually treated as silver and, in recent years, their history has been traced exhaustively by eminent silversmiths and other experts, notably:

(1) The late W. J. Cripps—*Old English Plate* (1878).
(2) The late W. H. St. John Hope—A paper on mazers read in January 1886 at a Society of Antiquaries meeting (vol. l, page 129).
(3) The late Sir Charles Jackson—*Illustrated History of English Plate* (1911).

I can add nothing to the full historical data already collated, but I must describe mazers somewhat lengthily to dispel the confusion which, mainly due to St. John Hope, has arisen regarding variety of wood and part of tree used and the reason for the peculiar shape of mazers. This confusion was unfortunately accentuated by the late Owen Evan-Thomas in *Domestic Utensils of Wood*.

As mentioned in the introduction, the history of treen is largely that of turning and, except for methers and certain types of coopered drinking vessels, most others are turnery. By the thirteenth century, probably much earlier, demand had arisen for ceremonial or community drinking vessels of wood and this set the turners a problem.

Until the seventeenth century probably, only home grown hardwoods were available and as sycamore, which now grows to greater size and perfection here than elsewhere, is a naturalised tree, believed to have been introduced in the sixteenth century, earlier turners had no suitable wood for making large drinking vessels.

Alternating periods of wetness and dryness create severe stresses in a wooden bowl, due to it being wet inside and dry outside when in use, with periods of alternating dryness and wetness of both sides, resulting from washing and drying after use. Moreover, it has to be turned to a fine limit to serve its purpose elegantly and comfortably. No English hardwood trees, which grow to large size, such as oak, elm, ash or beech, combine the qualities of freedom from warping and splits, sound heart, toughness, denseness of grain and consequent lack of undue porosity. When "turned" with the grain running vertically, large vessels made from these woods, however well seasoned, would leak badly from the base. If "turned" with the grain running horizontally, they would gradually become oval, as wood has negligible longitudinal but fairly considerable width shrinkage, varying according to species and degree of seasoning before "turning". This tendency of ovalness would mar appearance, debar the use of silver mounts and seriously affect the fit of the lid commonly used on important drinking vessels, to prevent introduction of poison or stop contamination. The unfortunate turners, therefore, were in a dilemma and their thoughts naturally turned to maple, a wood notoriously impermeable to liquids and one of the densest and sometimes most beautifully bird's-eye marked of our small but commonly growing hardwoods. It suited their purpose perfectly, except for size. Now maple is particularly prone to develop "burrs" or "burls", which are wart-like excrescences on the trunk, formed by growth round a wound or dormant buds; clusters of these gradually form solid, shallow curved protuberances, often of considerable diameter, particularly where they occur on the "butt"—that is, the junction of trunk and root. A small burr, hollowed to form a snuff box, but otherwise in its natural state, is in PLATE 55. Sometimes burrs are induced artificially by felling trees, the stumps of which then "stool": that is, they emit new shoots or twigs which are broken off and, when grown over, form burrs. Growth of burr wood is irregular, contorted and embraces what are actually clusters of knots; burr differs entirely in structure from both normal long grain and cross section. It produces very beautiful mottled figure and has always been prized, particularly for veneers. Because of this tangled, interwoven structure and lack of continuous straight grain in any direction, burrs, when hollowed out, have little movement in any direction and they proved the answer to the turners' prayers and ideal for mazers. Their only disadvantage—shallowness—was overcome in large and fine specimens by adding deep silver rims, which increased their depth. Incidentally, Part 6 indicates how the French in the eighteenth century solved their problem of making circular snuff boxes in the same manner as the thirteenth-century turners had done and in the nineteenth century burry roots proved the ideal material for bowls of pipes, whilst in this century the Japanese still make rice bowls of burry roots, turned in mazer form.

The word "mazer" appears to be derived from the old German word "masa", meaning a spot and speck (the origin of "measles"), and "maserle," the maple tree. Mazer, therefore, originally denoted the speckled wood from which the drinking bowls were made.

My careful investigation into "mazer wood" was prompted by obvious inconsistencies and contradictions in Owen Evan-Thomas' description, mostly a transcript of St. John Hope. Evan-Thomas says:

(1)   "Of all the drinking vessels in use from the 13th to the 16th century, none were so common and so much prized as those known as mazers."

He gives no explanation of this curious statement: common objects are rarely much prized, but the origin of this sentence has an explanation which I will detail later.

(2)   "In wills and inventories they were occasionally referred to as 'ciphi' or 'cuppa de mazer', 'mazeri', 'ciphi murrei', etc.; but whatever it is called, it is quite clear that the same vessel is meant, viz., a drinking bowl turned out of some kind of wood, but preferably maple, and especially the spotted or speckled variety called *bird's-eye maple*.[1]
     "Although the term 'mazer' is applied to a drinking bowl, it is from the material, and not from the use of the bowl, that the name is derived. The bole of the maple tree, or the part where several branches meet, was preferred by the turners as yielding the speckled grain known as bird's eye."

To this may largely be attributed the confusion which has arisen. Though to the uninitiated there may be resemblance between "spots" of bird's-eye and "spots" of burr, it is very superficial. The causes of burr and of bird's-eye markings are entirely different. Bird's-eye, by no means a rarity like burr, occurs commonly in maple and is caused by the action of a fungus in the cambium layer, that part of the tree immediately under the bark, in which active growth occurs. Consequently, bird's-eye can and sometimes does occur throughout the greater part or whole of a tree.

(3)   "The five characteristics of the mazer are: (i) the bowl, (ii) the band, (iii) the 'print', (iv) the foot, (v) the lid; but in most cases the last two never existed."

If the last two never existed, then how could they be characteristics?

Until now, these errors of Evan-Thomas are due to accepting St. John Hope without reasoning or investigation, but for the next, Evan-Thomas alone is responsible.

(4)   "The making of the true mazer bowl appears to have been discontinued about the last quarter of the 17th century, and much larger and deeper bowls of lignum vitæ and other hard woods took their place. The adoption of this species of wood, largely imported from South America and the West Indies, *enabled the bowls to be made deeper than did maple wood*,[1] as the deepest known mazer of maple wood is only four inches in depth, a fact which may be attributed to the limitation of the wood rather than to abstemiousness on the part of the revellers of the Plantagenet and the Tudor periods."

Now mazers exist slightly over 12 in. in diameter and if made from ordinary bird's-eye figured bole of maple, turned with the grain running horizontally, they could still be at least 6 in. deep. If, alternatively, they were "turned" with the grain running vertically, there was no practical limit to their depth or height. Evan-Thomas' explanation is unacceptable: the shape of mazers is governed by the general shape of burrs, usually from butts or roots, and they were chosen from there because (a) maple being a small tree in England, only the root would provide burr wood sufficiently large for ceremonial drinking vessels; (b) they were the most stable part of the tree for turning and mounting; (c) they showed beautiful markings, and (d) they were rare and worthy of mounting in precious metal.

After reading Evan-Thomas, I commenced a careful study of some extant mazers and obtained permission to examine closely those in the British Museum, the Victoria

---

[1] Author's italics.

and Albert Museum, St. Nicholas Hospital, Harbledown, the Worshipful Company of Vintners and various other collections. All I examined are made from burrs, burry butts or burry roots, with considerable variation in proportion of burr figure to that of root grain, but none is bird's-eye. I think it probable, but not certain, that all are maple. Nothing but removal of slices of the burr for microscopic examination could settle this last point and even then, owing to the curious structure of burrs and ravages of age, such examination would not always be conclusive.

As a further check, I had made, in a special manner, to my own design, a bowl of bird's-eye maple, in general outline resembling a mazer, in order to check whether the finished product showed any resemblance in marking to any mazer I had examined. The result is the interesting example of modern treen, one from the right (14). Even allowing for comparison of new with old, none of the grain or "spot" markings bears the slightest resemblance to "mazer" wood, although to introduce as much variety of bird's-eye as possible, the bowl has been built up in height out of five 1-in. layers of maple, glued together with synthetic resin adhesive. The joints of the four layers comprising the bowl are hidden externally by turned "reeds" and the fifth layer forms the foot. The diameter of the bowl is $11\frac{1}{2}$ in., height $4\frac{1}{4}$ in. It now only remains for someone to prove that mazers really were made of bird's-eye maple by rediscovering this bowl a few hundred years hence!

Sir Charles Jackson's monumental *History of English Plate* yielded nothing of interest on this aspect of mazers because the author states frankly, "The greater part of this chapter is taken from a paper by Mr. W. H. St. Hope John . . ."; then follows the same confusion about bird's-eye and burr and characteristics of mazers, identically as Evan-Thomas quoted later.

Jackson's source of information, St. John Hope, obviously had doubts about "the five characteristics" for, after describing them, he proceeds to say:

> "The only essential part of a mazer being its bowl, it is clear that the vessel would be complete in itself if all or any of the last four features were omitted . . . the cheaper form of mazer, or that in use among the poorer classes, would usually be but a plain bowl, while the wealthier folk ornamented their mazers with silver gilt mounts and enamelled medallions and occasionally with splendid feet and covers."

As the result of a reference in St. John Hope's paper, I read Cripps' book and was amazed to find that in 1878 he had reached conclusions, resulting from historical research, which coincided exactly with what I have rediscovered independently by tackling the investigation as a student of wood. Lack of space forbids my quoting Cripps here, but his corroborative evidence will be found between pages 178–81 of *Old English Plate* (1881).

On the subject of mazer wood, it only remains to add that in Devonshire the black cherry is called a mazer tree and that the *Oxford Dictionary* states "*mazer*, excrescence on a tree, maple, drinking-cup, etc. 1. A hard wood (?prop. maple) used as a material for drinking-cups. b. The tree yielding this (rare)—1547. 2. A bowl, drinking-cup, or goblet without a foot, orig. made of mazer wood. Often applied to bowls entirely of metal, etc."

I consider that the word "mazer" originally meant the burry excrescence of a maple tree but probably soon included other burry roots; next it changed to a drinking vessel made from maple or other burr and finally, in its broadest sense, it described a certain shape of bowl, not necessarily of wood. There are many analogous changes of meaning in the English language. Candlestick is typical: first a pointed stick on which a candle was impaled; then a pricket on a stand of wood; next a wooden cup on stem and foot and finally a cup on stem and foot made from any material, more often not wood.

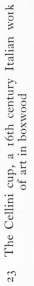

23   The Cellini cup, a 16th century Italian work of art in boxwood

22   The Hickman Chalice, a James I standing cup of fruitwood, with incised branded ornament and inscription

21   A rare Elizabethan standing cup of sycamore, with a set of Roundels in the base

25   The McIntosh loving cup.   A silver mounted coconut dated 1710

24   A silver mounted coconut goblet dated 1669 carved with incidents of the flight of Charles after the battle of Worcester

Mazers are the most important early drinking vessels of which a fair number survives and the large ones seem to have been the most valued wooden bowls in use between A.D. 1250 and 1550 or 1600. Probably, however, wooden cups made from burrs were known many centuries earlier. The standing mazer form in silver was common in the Roman civilisation and although naturally no small Roman articles of wood have survived, we know from Pliny that rare and costly wood veneers were used, so doubtless the Romans realised the value of burrs for making bowls.

As well as being called "myrrhine" and "de murro", mazers are referred to in wills and inventories as "cuppa de mazer" or "mazeri". It is interesting that inventories of monastic houses recorded the following figures at the dates quoted:

1328	Canterbury	.	.	.	182 mazers.
1437	Battle	.	.	.	32 mazers.
1446	Durham	.	.	.	49 mazers.
1540	Waltham	.	.	.	15 mazers.
1540	Westminster	.	.	.	40 mazers.

Not all these would have been large mazers, holding half a gallon or more; the majority would have been small individual bowls, for use by monks. These small mazers were probably the ones made from burrs formed at the part where several branches meet and they were the plain ones, referred to as "murræ usuales", as against the "murræ magnæ et largæ". This division of mazers into two distinct classes accounts for small ones being "common" and large ones "much prized".

Mazers are now very rare and most of the 60 or 70 that are known are amongst the most cherished possessions of church, universities and museums.

I see no justification for believing in "the five characteristics". Doubtless many, probably the majority, of mazers were simple, shallow bowls of maple burr, without the fashionable mounts, prints, feet or lids. Bearing in mind how long ago they were made, it is not surprising that only elaborate ones have survived or that, in most cases, only these were considered worthy of mention in mediæval inventories and wills.

Most mazers still extant are rimmed or banded and mounted on foot bands of silver or sometimes silver gilt. They have a circular medallion on the interior base, which was known in the fourteenth and fifteenth centuries as the "founce" or "frounce" and from the fifteenth century until the Reformation, as the "print". Some authorities consider that it was inserted to conceal the lathe mark, which was not obviated until the chuck was invented, whilst others assert that it was derived from the umbilical boss found in Greek pateræ and early Egyptian bowls. Some "prints" are engraved or embossed with portraits of the Virgin, others with coats of arms, stars or animals. Some surviving mazers, particularly later ones, are provided with two silver handles, affixed to straps connecting rims with bases.

The largest mazer now known is the Great Mazer at York, $12\frac{5}{8}$ in. in diameter but only $3\frac{1}{2}$ in. deep inside the bowl. It has an English inscription on the band. Other famous specimens include the "St. Bede's Bowl" at Durham and the "Guy of Warwick Mazer" at Harbledown. The latter, which dates between 1307 and 1327, has its print decorated with a picture of Sir Guy Warwick on horseback, pinning down with his spear a dragon which is on its back.

Sixteenth-century mazers are usually deeper, being more heavily mounted than earlier ones. PLATE 15 illustrates a fine specimen, and PLATE 16 its print. This mazer from Epworth church, Lincolnshire, is a recent acquisition of the British Museum. It has silver mounts and a print, at one time enamelled, with engraved figures of St. John the Baptist and St. Andrew, the saint to whom the church is dedicated. The bowl, of maple root with an all-over small burr marking, has a diameter of $6\frac{7}{8}$ in. and inside depth of $1\frac{1}{4}$ in. The silver mount increases its diameter to $8\frac{3}{4}$ in., its inside depth to $2\frac{3}{4}$ in. and outside depth to 3 in. I do not consider that this bowl ever had a foot. It has a slight rim under it, formed in order to give it a flat base. The thickness of this rim slightly exceeds $\frac{1}{16}$ in. and forms a circle $3\frac{3}{4}$ in. in diameter, which shows considerable signs of wear and is the same colour as the remainder of the bowl. It is quite round on the edge and could have provided no fixing for the rivets of a mount. Moreover, it is recessed in the centre for the rivet of the print and this recessing for rivet and washer would have been unnecessary if they were going inside a hollow foot.

In addition to mazer bowls with and without feet, some mounted on stems were made. Probably always rare, few have survived. They are known as standing mazers. It is believed that only three English specimens with original feet now exist. Commander How, who has added considerably to our knowledge of Scottish standing mazers (see "Scottish Standing Mazers" by Commander G. E. P. How, F.A.S. Scot., *Proceedings of the Society of Antiquaries of Scotland*, vol. lxviii (vol. viii, Sixth Series), 1933–34, pages 394–411), has revealed records of several Scottish examples and I am indebted to him for the illustration of one of the finest, "The Tulloch Mazer" (18). Its dimensions are:

Across bowl	.	.	.	$7\frac{7}{8}$ inches.
Height	.	.	.	$7\frac{7}{8}$ inches.
Across base	.	.	.	$5\frac{5}{8}$ inches.
Depth of bowl	.	.	.	$2\frac{3}{8}$ inches.

Commander How states:

"It is at present the earliest hall-marked definitely ascribed example of Scottish silver. The mounts are of silver-gilt, the band being decorated with engraved scroll foliage and human figures. The stem of the cup is chased with floral ornament . . . Thanks to the very important work recently carried out by Miss Wood on the Old Canongate records . . . I am now able to state that from these records, in 1569, there were six goldsmiths working in the Canongate, amongst them James Gray and one John Acheson, styled 'Maister Cungyear' (that is Master Coiner) to the King. There can be no doubt that this James Gray, who designed the memorial to the Regent Murray in St. Giles' Cathedral, was the maker of both the Tulloch and the Galloway mazers . . .

"The print of the Tulloch mazer is of very exceptional interest, having been . . . originally enamelled.

"The arms are those of Tulloch of Tannochy, with the inscription: 'HONORA DEUM EX TOTA ANIMA TUA', and the date 1557, which places this mazer as having been made when 'Bloody' Mary was on the throne of England . . .'"

For comparison of form, note the unusual seventeenth-century simple standing cup, without mounts (right, 14). It is beautifully faded and has the bowl and foot of some burry root, closely resembling amboyna; the stem is yew. The knop on the baluster stem (the reverse way up to that on all recorded standing mazers) gives a particularly satisfying hand grip. It measures 6 in. across; its height is 7 in. and depth 2 in.

Even rarer than the mazer is a closely allied drinking vessel, sometimes called a double mazer, of which few examples have survived. Its shape resembles a small "cottage loaf" and it is usually made from maple burr but, like the mazer, examples occur wholly of silver. Three vessels are shown in German heraldry and illuminations of the fifteenth century and it appears likely that these curious creations are the German equivalent of mazers, notwithstanding some being in English collections and bearing English coats of arms. The upper half of the "loaf" forms the cover or tasting cup and is usually surmounted by a pierced silver coronet, which forms a foot when the cover is inverted for use as a taster. The lower and larger "loaf" shaped bowl has a single upturned handle at the side and is mounted on another pierced silver stand, which sometimes has three feet in addition.

Another unusual and beautiful form of German mazer, made about 1500, appears in PLATE 17. Its shape appears to have been dictated largely by the burr formation which is exceptionally clearly defined and beautifully marked. It is in one piece and the eight-foil edge encloses a circular bowl. At one side the burr extends outwards, forming a scallop-edged handle. The foot, rim and print are silver-gilt. Between the lobes of the rim are silver bosses of curly leaves, which match in character the rosette "print".

In the seventeenth century true mazers seem to have died out, their place being taken by deeper bowls or cups, some with and some without stems and often with silver-mounted feet and rims. They were usually known as mazer cups and mostly were of beech or pear.

A seventeenth-century, simply mounted pearwood standing cup of this type—unusual because fitted with a nest of five tumblers—is in PLATE 19. These "tumblers", with rounded bases, really did tumble; hence one origin of our word "tumbler".

The transition between true mazers and these mazer cups shows clearly in two rare seventeenth-century lignum vitæ drinking bowls (left, 14). Deeper in proportion to diameter than normal mazers and their walls unusually thin, they retain the mazer foot and, contrary to usual European practice, where diameter exceeds height, are turned with the grain running vertically. They are probably two early English essays in "turning" this then newly imported wood. The larger, which has warped badly, is $5\frac{1}{2}$ in. in diameter and $2\frac{1}{2}$ in. inside depth. The lignum vitæ bowl, shown on edge, with circular aperture in base, is a problem. The opening is "threaded" and may have held a silver "print", to which was attached a stem and foot, or it may have taken a strainer or spout.

WASSAIL BOWLS—The seventeenth century saw the introduction of community type wassail or "lambs wool" bowls—large receptacles intended for holding drink, not drinking vessels like mazers.

Manufacture was made possible by the introduction at that time of lignum vitæ, the only tree, known then, sufficiently large without jointing to provide a bowl up to 15 or 16 in. in diameter and sufficiently durable, sound of heart and dense grained to be "turned" with the grain running vertically. This wood, one of the hardest, densest and most resistant to decay known, comes from the West Indies and coastal districts of tropical America. The first European to report it was Oviedo, who found it in St. Domingo in 1514. Its importation on a commercial scale removed all practical limit on size of bowls or drinking vessels, for it turns beautifully, while at the time of its introduction, though seldom now, it was available in diameters up to at least 18 in. Its markings, too, are extremely beautiful for turnery, which shows up its dark greenish brown or near-black heartwood, sharply defined from the yellowish sapwood. As it was also supposed to possess magical medicinal properties and had, in fact, been introduced to Europe early in the sixteenth century for that reason, not surprisingly it became the most popular wood for high grade drinking vessels. According to Fluckiger and Hanbury (*Pharmacographia*, 1879) treatises on this wood were written in Germany in 1517, 1518 and 1519. The last, which gives a tolerable description of the tree, its wood bark and medicinal properties, was translated into English in 1533. It was published in London in 1536 under the title *Of the wood called Guaiacum that healeth the Frenche Pockes and also helpeth the gout in the feete, the stoone, the palsey, lepree, dropsy, fallynge euyll and other diseases.*

Smaller wassail drinking bowls go back to Saxon times and to the Saxons we owe the words "waes hael" meaning "be whole" or "be well". One of the earliest references to wassailing in English history is in the days of Vortigern, King of Britain; at his reception by the Saxon King, Hengist, the latter's daughter, the Princess Rowena, is related to have "come unto the king's presence with a cup of gold filled with wine in her hand and, making a low reverence unto the king said 'Waes hael hlaford cyning,' 'Be of health, Lord King' ".

Judging by the number surviving, lignum vitæ bowls must have been made in large quantities, but rarely two alike. They were usually but not invariably mounted on a centre stem and circular foot. This in turn rested in a turned tray on which was arrayed a number of small turned tumblers or dippers of similar wood and pattern. I have a rare seventeenth-century specimen, $11\frac{1}{4}$ in. in diameter, which has no stem or foot and has never had either. Some of the more elaborate bowls were silver-mounted and covered by a lid on which was a centre stem surmounted by a smaller replica of the lower bowl; this acted as a spice box and contained a grater for the nutmegs used in the spicing or mulling of the beverages. Occasionally the lid also had stands for dippers or tumblers. Three fine seventeenth-century wassail bowls are in PLATE 20. The first is of finely marked lignum vitæ, with two well defined turned bands; it is $7\frac{1}{2}$ in. high and $6\frac{1}{2}$ in. in diameter. The second is also of lignum vitæ, with a slightly tapering bowl. Its height is 9 in. and diameter $8\frac{3}{4}$ in. The third, of yew wood, is of most attractive colour and form and is ornamented with four circular bands turned from the solid; its height is $7\frac{1}{4}$ in. and diameter $6\frac{1}{8}$ in.

Although, as already mentioned, lignum vitæ was imported to Europe in the sixteenth century, its use at first appears to have been confined to medicinal purposes and I wonder whether wassail bowls of this wood, ascribed as A.D. 1600, 1620 and 1640, were really made as early, although based on design and on engine-turned ornament especially, they appear correctly dated. They may well be examples of old design lingering on. I should be very interested to learn of a silver-mounted bowl of lignum vitæ bearing a hall-mark as early as 1670. My doubt arises because John Evelyn, the noted diarist who was particularly interested in wood and woodwork, does not appear to have mentioned these important vessels in his writings and, in his great work, *Sylva, or a Discourse of Forest Trees*, second edition (1670), he dismisses lignum vitæ briefly as ". . . fittest for the shrubby part and under-furniture of our evergreen groves and near our gardens of pleasure". As Evelyn specifically mentions purposes for which various trees were suited and used and refers to such woods as yew and box for bowls and drinking vessels, it seems unlikely that lignum vitæ could have been used much at that time for turnery.

The capacity of the largest vessels was up to five gallons, so it would have required two men to lift one when full and it was the fashion for those present to take their part in mixing the "punch" in the bowl, which was filled at table and kept in one place from which it was emptied by wooden dippers or ladles. At least one large seventeenth-century wassail bowl still exists which had three silver taps in the sides for emptying it, but the dirty habit of using a dipper was common practice. In the eighteenth century ladles of the type in PLATE 48 came into common use.

The alternative name of "lambs wool" bowl arose from the froth on the surface of the drink, which was known as lamb's wool. The ingredients seem to have varied considerably but always to have contained beaten up eggs, which created the frothy effect. References to "drinking lamb's wool" occur in a poem by Robert Herrick (1591–1674), in Samuel Pepys' diary for 1666 and 1667, in Oliver Goldsmith's *Vicar of Wakefield* and in Parson Woodforde's diary for 1775. In early days, the body of the drink seems to have been composed of ale flavoured with "bobbing apples" and spices.

Wassailing was especially a Shrove Tuesday and a Christmas custom. At the latter

26 Miscellaneous treen goblets, pocket spice boxes and two 18th century trays

27 An unusual 17th century tumbler cup with a whistle in the base

28 A silver mounted quaich of 1692

29 Georgian decanter stand, coasters, bottle stands, and staved wine cooler of bucket form

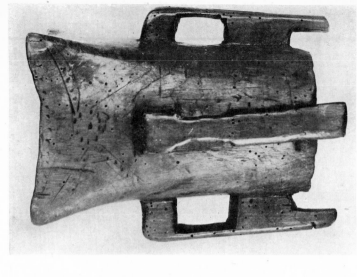

31 A mediæval Irish mether cut from the solid.
    Drinking was from the angle spouts of these
    awkward vessels

30 17th or early 18th century Irish lámhógs, hollowed from solid blocks of willow

the wassail bowl, decked with ribbons and rosemary, was carried through country villages until comparatively recently, the maidens carrying the bowl singing carols.

HANAPS OR STANDING CUPS—The most decorative and among the rarest drinking vessels ever made were standing cups, formerly called hanaps and mostly fitted with covers. As early as the eleventh century they were the grand drinking cups. John of Gaunt in 1394 bequeathed his finest hanap of gold. In Calthrop's reports of 1670 we find "he which is mayor of London for the time shall have an hanap d'or". The receptacle for holding the hanap, when not in use, was called a hanaper, now corrupted into our word "hamper". Most of the cups surviving date from James I. They are of silver, wood, coconut and ostrich eggs; some of the former may have been used as chalices in private chapels, but others were intended for secular use. The wooden cups were usually beech, sycamore or pear, decorated with incised branded ornamentation and occasionally with engraved silver mounts in addition, similar to those used for coconuts and ostrich eggs. Early seventeenth-century treen standing cups are much rarer than silver. Only about fourteen genuine specimens are known; most are dated. Their ornament usually includes the Royal or other coats of arms and frequently outlines of animals, such as stags, lions, unicorns, etc. A feature of seventeenth-century specimens is the long semi-religious and rather sanguinary inscriptions which are engraved round cup and foot rims and sometimes under bases.

Some, known as steeple cups, have the knops or knobs of their covers terminating in a steeple. The knobs sometimes open, disclosing hollow receptacles for spices. This feature was also known in the sixteenth century, as in the very rare Elizabethan cup (21). Of sycamore, decorated on the surface with bands of ornaments in sunk relief, the lower part of the tapering base forms a box containing ten Cedar of Lebanon roundels. The upper portion of the base is hollow, forming a receptacle for a lemon. Inverted, it forms a stand for the stoneware pot in which posset was heated over the fire. Above this base is the cup proper, in this instance a double cup, the smaller (lower) one fitting into a socket round the lemon box, the larger (upper) cup having a domed lid projecting beyond the rim of the cup which contains the spice. Surmounting this is a small cup which acts as the lid handle; its lower part also forms a cover for the spice-box and the outer portion is hollowed to contain a nutmeg. When completely assembled, it forms an imposing table ornament, 18 in. high and $4\frac{5}{16}$ in. in diameter.

A magnificent James I standing cup of fruitwood (22), known as the "Hickman Chalice", consists of a deep, turned bowl on a stem with wide, flattened knop and spreading foot. On the hatched ground round the bowl near the lip is a diamond pattern, and a deep band of continuous leaf ornament, cross-hatched and much stylised, round the body of the bowl. The same pattern occurs on the foot. Under the lip-band and continued round the foot of the bowl is the inscription:

"The Lord of Lyfe his Precious Blood hath shed from Death and Hell his chosen to redeeme such as from Sinne are risen from the dead him and his word they greatly do esteeme for that from so great Death they are set free they shune all Sinne and serve him thankfully."

Round the foot is another inscription:

"God's word sincerely often preached and read, true Christian Soules it doth in ofte truly feed. Thereby they learn a Blessed lyfe to leade: to them Christ giveth worty Drink indeede: his owne Deare Bloud."

Under the foot, in concentric circles, is the continued inscription:

"Doth cleanse them all Sinne. Salvation Good they so are sure to Winne: Because they do feel the Power of Christes Death working in them effectually the Death of all Sinne and the Power of his resurrection raising them up to newness of lyfe to serve God with a faithfull sincere loving and obedient heart so rune that you may obtain: 1608."

The cover is dome-shaped with double baluster finial and ornamental band matching that on the bowl. The dimensions are: height, with cover, 13 in., diameter of bowl 5¼ in., depth 4½ in.

Bowls and standing cups without covers, but with similar ornament, are encountered occasionally.

A magnificent work of art, formed as a standing cup (23), is a sixteenth-century Renaissance example attributed to Benvenuto Cellini. It is of finely patinated boxwood, the colour of cornelian. Dimensions are:

Overall height	. . .	15¼ inches.
Diameter	. . .	5 inches.
Height, without lid	. .	9¾ inches.
Depth of bowl	. .	4¼ inches.
Internal diameter	. . .	4⅜ inches.

The whole conception certainly suggests the work of a superb artist in ivory or precious metal.

The lid is finely decorated with trophies and surmounted by the winged lion of Venice, holding a coat of arms. Between the two guilloche bandings on the cup is a frieze, exquisitely carved with allegorical scenes, featuring cherubs in clouds—one, Cupid, is shooting a love arrow at a couple seated on a dolphin in the waves, which encircle the base of the frieze. Of the other nudes, some ride sea horses whilst others are carried by winged dolphins over the waves. Under the lower guilloche band are shell-shaped lozenges, separated by bearded heads. The lozenges, four in number, each contains scenes with Neptune or other mythological marine figures. The knop on the stem is carved with figures and the inner ring of the base with minute scenes with a sea background. The outer ring has trophies of musical instruments and armour, separated by festoons of fruit and flowers.

Standing cups and mazers are among the few varieties of treen sufficiently valuable to have aroused the faker's cupidity and collectors must guard against wholly spurious examples and made-up pieces and old vessels to which later ornament has been added.

COCONUTS—Coconuts were used considerably as drinking vessels and their introduction must have been regarded as providential in view of their natural form being ideal for drinking cups. Their low porosity and easiness for carving, polishing, drilling and mounting were additional assets. Apart from price, their only disadvantage was brittleness, which applies to all nut shells, owing to absence of long grain fibres.

Coconuts were often elaborately carved and silver mounted for protection and used as the bodies of jugs and bowls of standing cups from the thirteenth to the eighteenth centuries. The pointed end invariably forms the base, the rounded end being removed because the eyes constitute a weakness.

The Glasgow Art Gallery and Museums possess a magnificent Charles II silver-mounted coconut goblet. It is divided by narrow silver bands into three panels, illustrating incidents in the flight of Charles after the Battle of Worcester. In one panel, the King's head and that of Col. Carles peer from the foliage of the Boscobel oak, while two Cromwellian troopers ride below. A ribbon stretches across the tree trunk, bearing the picture of the three Crowns and the inscription "1000 PVND-FDK". The second panel depicts the King, dressed as a servant, riding into a pond near a castellated house, while a man whips on the horse. The third panel (24) shows the King on horseback with Mrs. Jane Lane, who assisted his escape, seated behind him. The silver rim is dated 1669.

The McIntosh cup (25), a loving-cup formerly in the possession of Commander How, is a fine example of an early eighteenth-century silver-mounted coconut. It is particularly well documented from records in the Inverness Register of "Sasines" (Acts giving possession of feudal property), is dated 1710 and inscribed on the foot "Gift Provost Duff to L.M.I.T. A.D." (the initials M.I.T. are intertwined and L.M.I.T. are over the initials A.D.). The gift was from the then Provost of Inverness to Lauchlan, 20th chief of McIntosh, on occasion of his marriage to Ann Duff, whose father was Provost of Inverness in 1715.

LOVING CUPS—As the last illustration shows, treen loving cups followed the outlines of goblets, but in larger form, as they were passed round the table and sipped by each guest in turn. They measured as much as 14 in. in height and were chiefly seventeenth- and eighteenth-century lignum vitæ products.

MISCELLANEOUS DRINKING VESSELS—In addition to the more ceremonial vessels so far described, there were also in common use, from earliest times, turned wooden drinking cups. Being of small value, no very early and common vessels have survived; we know little about them except that records usually describe them as "beechen". In the seventeenth and the first half of the eighteenth century, they were of lignum vitæ, sycamore, maple, cherry, pear, beech, holly, yew, etc. The majority were plain, though considerably varied in the shape of their turning, but a few were decorated with arms, crests, mottoes and verses, incised with a hot iron. In general, their design closely followed or was followed by cups of the same periods in metal and glass.

A drinking vessel to which mediæval documents sometimes refer was the piggin, a small wooden pail-like vessel with one stave longer than the rest, to serve as handle. The staves were bound with metal, cane or willow. The word piggin is a diminutive of pigskin, from which these vessels were first made. Old documents relate that there were four degrees of drunkenness, of which "pig drunk" was the worst. Long after it had fallen into disuse as a drinking vessel, in fact right up to this century, the piggin has continued in the dairy as a milk ladling vessel (see Part 5).

In PLATE 26 is a selection of simple stemmed goblets, from the seventeenth century onwards. The goblet on the extreme left is curious in as much as the bowl has an outside depth of 3½ in. but an inside depth of only 2 in. The explanation may be that it was designed for an abstemious host, wishing to "fill up" each time with his guests, without drinking much himself. The crude elm goblet in the background is a Welsh cottage specimen, used until recently. On the oval tray are four varied goblets and in front of it two more, whose dates cannot be established with certainty. Second from the left on the tray is a yew wood goblet in the style of glass of 1700. Next, the ebony goblet is probably eighteenth century, whilst the olivewood specimen (right), despite being copied from a 1680 design, appears to be nineteenth century. The miniature barrel and the bottle on the tray, as also the engine-turned "trick" ball in front, are all eighteenth-century pocket spice boxes, with graters inside.

The curious vessel with small cup and tall stem is believed to be a seventeenth-century wine "biber", used in the cellar for tasting wine from the cask. The two finely turned mahogany goblets on the piecrust tray are 6 in. high and date from 1760–90. In the foreground is a modern combination cork borer and tap.

IRISH DRINKING VESSELS—Lámhógs and methers, two distinctive types of crude wooden drinking vessels, originated in Ireland. Methers were used, it is believed, from the fourteenth to the seventeenth century, whilst lámhógs continued up to this century. Four lámhógs, in some districts called piggins, are in PLATE 30. These are probably seventeenth- or early eighteenth-century specimens, made from willow, which shared favour for these vessels with elm, beech and ash. They are capacious: the largest, $8\frac{1}{2}$ in. high by $6\frac{1}{2}$ in. diameter, holds three pints; the two medium ones, $7\frac{1}{4}$ in. high by 5 in. diameter, each holds $1\frac{3}{4}$ pints. The smallest bears the Gaelic inscription "Céad míle fáilte" (ten thousand welcomes), is $5\frac{3}{4}$ in. high by 4 in. diameter and holds over $\frac{3}{4}$ pint. It was incorrectly described by Evan-Thomas in *Domestic Utensils of Wood* as a "mether" cup. Lámhógs were hollowed from solid blocks on a pole lathe and doubtless partially turned externally by the same means. They must have been finished with hand tools, as the handles are cut from the same block as the vessel. Lámhógs were sometimes imported from Ireland into West of England taverns.

The second type of cup, the mether, differs considerably from the lámhóg in as much as it is rectangular in section at rim and usually rounded at base, although there also it sometimes approaches the rectangular. Moreover, in methers the base is usually inserted as a separate unit and sometimes there are two handles, sometimes four and often none. Cambridge possesses a mether and the National Museum, Dublin, has several, of which a willow specimen is shown in PLATE 31. It is $8\frac{1}{2}$ in. high and $4\frac{3}{4}$ in. wide at the top. The four handles, carved from the solid, project about $\frac{3}{4}$ in. below the bottom, to serve as feet. This mether is unusual in having an incised pokerwork decoration on it of the emasculated interlacing variety common in the mediæval centuries when the full flower of Irish interlacing had decayed. Drinking must have taken place from the spouts formed by the angles of the concave sides of these awkward vessels, of which little authenticated archæological information is available. Those which have survived are valuable rarities.

The name mether is often said to be derived from the herb drink mead, medd or meodu, which consisted of rosemary, hissop, thyme, etc., boiled with honey, but no evidence has been produced to support this.

SCOTTISH DRINKING VESSELS—Independence is a Scottish characteristic and this trait shows in the development of their fine drinking treen. Formerly two distinct forms were used—"cuachs" or "quaichs", which were shallow bowls, and the "bicker" family, which also included "cogs" or "coggies" and "luggies". These latter were straight-sided vessels, related in origin of form and name to our beakers. Considerable numbers of these vessels are in public collections in Scotland, but they are becoming "finds" for collectors. A selection is in PLATE 28 and PLATE 32.

Most of these vessels were coopered and characterised by alternate staves of light and dark wood which, allied with good workmanship, makes them extremely decorative and, without being too fanciful, is reminiscent of the Scottish pleated tartan. This resemblance is heightened sometimes by bases and more rarely sides being divided into alternating squares of light and dark wood.

When these vessels were first used is unknown; it may have been in the seventeenth century or earlier, but roughly their known period covers the eighteenth and nineteenth centuries. In the National Museum of Antiquities of Scotland there is a luggie made at Cumbernauld as late as 1883. In the painting "The Penny Wedding," belonging to H.M. the King, painted by Sir David Wilkie in 1818, is depicted a fine selection of Scottish drinking treen. A "penny wedding" was a marriage festival, once common in Scotland, at which each guest contributed to the festive expenses, the surplus going to the newly married couple. The painted scene shows the wedding festival in a barn and in the foreground is a three-handled "quaich" and a large "coggie" with a ladle in it. A man is pouring drink from an oak-jack into a bi-coloured staved "bicker"; there is a "luggie" on a dresser and numerous other staved vessels are stored on shelves on the walls and among the rafters.

"Bickers" and "cogs" or "coggies" are the straight-sided staved vessels in PLATE 32, which have two of the staves curved outwards horizontally at the top to form concave handles. The definitions of "bickers" and "cogs" are vague: "cogs" are described as large "bickers", but as "bickers" are made in numerous sizes, it is impossible to define where one variety ends and the other begins. My smallest "bicker", that on the right, is $1\frac{7}{8}$ in. high and $2\frac{1}{16}$ in. diameter at top, excluding handles. The next size is $2\frac{1}{4}$ in. high and $3\frac{3}{8}$ in. diameter at top, while the two large ones, which possibly should be described as "cogs", are $3\frac{3}{8}$ in. high and $5\frac{1}{4}$ in. diameter at top excluding handles, which always occur on the light coloured staves. The vessel of piggin type, with one stave carried upwards to form a lug or handle, was known as a "luggie" and was really a porringer, not a drinking vessel. Some of these luggies, including the specimen illustrated, have a double base with a pea inserted in the cavity, so that a child could rattle the luggie when requiring more porridge.

Whilst small bickers were definitely drinking vessels, some cogs, like luggies, were used as porringers and very large cogs and vessels of similar construction but with two lugs, like the specimen left of PLATE 32, were set central on the table and used as communal porridge or kale bowls, as well as for holding milk or ale and for filling bickers. In their largest form they were merely well constructed buckets, made from two-coloured staves.

Now examine the construction. These vessels, which are completely watertight, are supposed to have been made with a pocket-knife as sole tool; there are few craftsmen to-day who could create such beautiful bowls with a full kit of tools. Observe the "cog" with interior showing and note that every stave is "feathered" into its two neighbours with never more nor less than five feathers. The four sections of the bottom are cross-tongued into each other and the jointing of the willow banding on the best specimens is a miracle of neatness. It was no mean feat of geometrical drawing either to "set-out" these tapered bowls so that each stave was of identical size, except in those examples which were made deliberately with their handled staves extra wide.

Not only is there confusion between "bickers" and "cogs", but also between "bickers" and "quaichs", small bickers sometimes being called quaichs. This is not surprising, as the Gaelic for both "cog" and "quaich" is "cuach". Generally, however, "quaich" is applied to the small shallow drinking vessels, resembling in form the silver bleeding bowl used in England and Holland in the seventeenth and eighteenth centuries.

A finely feathered staved "quaich", of alternating light and dark woods, is in PLATE 28. It is hooped with cane, but has silver-mounted handles and a silver foot and print, as on some mazers. The "print" is engraved with the initials JR7, surmounted by a crown and the date 1692. Each handle bears the initials B.H. The diameter at lip is $4\frac{3}{4}$ in. Silver feet and prints are just as common on the best quaichs as they are on the best mazers, but quaichs being so much "later" than mazers, a number of unmounted specimens has survived.

Two spreading handles are usual on quaichs, but occasionally they have three or even four, and instead of being horizontal they sometimes curve downwards. The larger specimens were passed from hand to hand on festive occasions. The woods most usually employed for all these bi-coloured staved vessels are laburnum, mahogany or walnut for dark staves and sycamore (called in Scotland "plane") for light staves. The bandings are usually willow or cane, but specimens with iron, brass or silver hoops exist. Quaichs were copied in silver as early as the seventeenth century and initially the staved form was perpetuated by modelling the silver in simulation, which extended to copying bands and even feathering of staves. Some silver quaichs are plain, shallow silver bowls, sometimes with a raised "print" in the base. These, too, may have been copied from wood or the plain wooden quaichs cut from the solid may be copied from silver. A nineteenth-century specimen of this type, hollowed from oak and with a "print" formed by a silver coin of 1693, is in the front row (32). It is 3⅛ in. in diameter.

An unusual form of quaich is one of Prince Charlie's, formerly in Sir Walter Scott's collection. A copy is right of PLATE 32. It is walnut, divided by rims into three parallel circular troughs. The handles are carved from the solid. The outer and middle troughs are connected by holes bored through the dividing rim, thus controlling the flow. The small centre circle, which was never filled with liquid, has a glass spy panel on the bottom, inscribed "For its bottom is of glass that he who quaffed might keep his eye the while upon the dirk hand of his [adversary?]. This last word is not clear.

COOPERED VESSELS—Oak kegs have been made from early times in varying sizes. The most common is the harvest keg; harvest kegs are known alternatively as costrels, beaver barrels or beaver kegs. The willow-bound keg standing vertically in PLATE 33 is of the "Vivandière" type used during the Napoleonic wars and the horizontal one adjacent, with glass ends, is the "St. Bernard" pattern. Both are cane bound. The iron-bound keg behind, with two bands and a handle, is a nineteenth-century Welsh costrel. In England, these kegs were more often the shape of miniature barrels and until the beginning of this century, were used for carrying cider and beer to workers in the fields. Each keg had, fitted over the bung, an iron "tot", which acted as a drinking vessel. Most kegs have leather thong handles and a vent peg, which acts as a safety valve if the keg is shaken or stood in the sun. The owner's initials usually appear on one end.

On the right, the iron-bound oak barrel on stand is a sherry barrel of a type still used. The copper-banded oak bottle was probably made by one of the old coopers who specialised in the manufacture of oak "jacks" (jugs).

TUMBLERS—In addition to round-bottomed "tumblers", there were also those with a pointed base. A rare and unusual late seventeenth-century "tumbler" drinking cup, a walnut variant of this type, is in PLATE 27. It has a whistle in the base and an incised inscription reading:

> "*Take not from me all my store,*
> *Except you fill me with some more,*
> *For have to borrow and never to pay,*
> *I call that foul play.*
> —H. N. Watson, 1695."

The cup is 8 in. long by 3 in. diameter at the widest and 2¼ in. diameter inside; it holds ½ pint.

An example of a rare seventeenth-century walnut "tumbler" holder, formed rather like a standing salt, with the bowl hollowed deeply into a pointed cone shape for the early glass "tumblers", which were cut off where blown and ended in a point, is shown right of the salts in PLATE 6.

WINE COOLERS—In the eighteenth century the cabinetmaker was called in to assist and eventually partially superseded the turner and cooper in making specialised equipment associated with drink. Enclosed wine coolers in varied forms, usually of mahogany, were made *en suite* with other dining-room furniture by all the great designers.

Brass-bound staved mahogany ice pails and plate carriers were made *en suite* and occasionally eighteenth-century wine coolers of bucket form with alternate light and dark staves and brass bands and liners, like the attractive one in PLATE 29, are found. Top and bottom bands are original, but the centre one appears to have been added to replace four brass wires, the grooves for which show plainly.

COASTERS, BOTTLE STANDS AND TRAYS—The best eighteenth- and early nineteenth-century "coasters" or circular bottle and decanter stands revived two fashionable features of mazers—metal "prints" in the lignum vitæ or mahogany bases, and metal rims. Both silver and plate were used and in 400 years time, when humble specimens will doubtless have been destroyed, silver or plated prints and rims may be described as having been essential characteristics of true coasters! Simpler homes used japanned iron, papier-mâché and plain wood coasters and bottle stands; PLATE 29 shows a selection in treen. At the back left is a plain oak version of a nineteenth-century design which was made in considerable quantities in silver and plate. The turner has followed the fashion to the extent of turning a "print" in the oak base. The three shallower coasters are mahogany and date from the second half of the eighteenth century. That on the left is engine-turned, the centre one is plain and the one on the right has a Sheraton inlay banding round the rim. The deep mahogany and boxwood staved stand in front and the elm country-made "spindle frame" stand are both early nineteenth century and were often used for sauce bottles.

To left of the same picture is the predecessor of the Victorian "tantalus" stand, the much better designed Georgian stand for decanters and glasses. The example illustrated is a Sheraton piece of 1795–1800, is mahogany, with the central turned pillar handle and lines round the gallery and base of boxwood. The ebony pillars supporting the gallery have ivory finials and the gallery itself is pierced for three decanters, their stoppers and twelve glasses.

Serving as a receptacle for the two mahogany goblets (right, 26) is a charming little mahogany "piecrust" waiter, $9\frac{3}{4}$ in. in diameter. Its design recalls mahogany piecrust table tops and Georgian silver waiters and suggests 1725–45.

Both small circular Georgian "piecrust" trays and larger ovals are in demand to-day. Their high price has attracted the cupidity of the faker. The usual trick is to make them from old mahogany, often salvaged from tops of Victorian dining tables. The old top surface of the table forms the bottom of the tray and it looks and is a genuine old, faded mahogany. The other surface has to be destroyed in moulding the edging and hollowing the inside of the tray and, once you know this trick, the faker's work can be distinguished. Though he often fades the wood chemically and polishes it industriously, there is a distinct difference, both to eye and touch, between top and underside.

The $18\frac{1}{2}$ in. long oval coaster tray of about 1750 is well proportioned, with its rim made from thin coopered staves of mahogany, two of which are extended upwards and scrolled outwards to form handles. It is banded with brass.

RUNNING FOOTMAN'S STAFF—This was one of the most curious examples of treen connected with drinking. In the days of heavy coaches and narrow streets, wealthy men, when driving through towns, were preceded by a running footman, who cleared the way in streets where two coaches could not pass. The running footman carried a 6 or 7 ft. long pole or staff, the head of which contained a half gill glass of spirit, secured by the screw knob. The last man to employ a running footman was "Old Q". The only running footman now is the one who has achieved immortality as the sign of a Mayfair public house. Walking sticks similarly fitted, are found occasionally.

*　　　*　　　*

COLLECTORS NOTES

Many museums contain examples of drinking treen and some colleges, notably All Souls and Oriel, Oxford, have rare specimens of mazers and standing cups, but none, so far as I am aware, has a comprehensive collection of treen drinking vessels.

The Victoria and Albert and the British Museums both possess magnificent mazers and standing cups. The National Museum of Antiquities, Edinburgh, has excellent quaichs, bickers, etc. Glasgow Art Gallery and Museums, thanks to the munificence of Sir William Burrell, possess superb chalices, steeple cups, wassail bowls and other drinking vessels; it also has quaichs and bickers. St. Nicholas Hospital, Harbledown, has several fine mazers including the earliest specimen known. Dublin and Belfast have early methers and lámhógs. The National Museum of Wales has numerous simple treen goblets and costrels or harvest kegs. The last are in many museums including those at Lincoln, Luton, Brighton, Worthing, Horsham, Cambridge and County Folk Museum, etc.

German "cottage loaf" mazers are in the Wallace Collection and British Museum. Taunton Museum has the unique whistling cup illustrated and Gloucester Museum has an unusual cider coaster. In the private collection of Commander F. Hart, R.N. (Retd.), at Chipping Campden, is an interesting seventeenth-century cider or beer coaster. It consists of an oblong beech board, mounted on four wheels, with a large circular recess for a "Black Jack" and three smaller recesses for horn beakers.

The Haselmere Museum is the place in which to see Scandinavian tankards.

The Worshipful Company of Vintners possess a mazer and an oak "Jack" dated 1662.

32   Scottish drinking vessels.   Two quaichs and a selection of staved bickers and cogs, the staves are "feathered" into each other and willow bound

33   Coopered kegs and bottle

34   A large mixing bowl, and a rolling pin and potato masher *en suite*. Skimmer spoon, cabbage presser, handled bowl and Sussex dry storage jar. Front right, a rare and early tilting hob.

35   A steak beater, skimmer spoon, boxwood rolling pin and potato masher. Extreme right, a standing spice box. In front, two lemon squeezers

PART THREE

IN THE KITCHEN

NOW to the kitchen, one of the last strongholds of treen. Long after the virtual disappearance of treen drinking and eating vessels, beech and sycamore reigned in the kitchen. Many wooden objects, such as salt and spice boxes, flour barrels, egg racks and towel and pastry rollers, commonplace in our childhood, have since been superseded by newer materials. Soon the chopping board may be the only piece of kitchen treen.

Admittedly the departure of so much kitchen treen need cause no regret, for nowhere else in the house has greater improvement in appearance and hygiene been effected by introducing brighter and more impervious materials.

However, now is the time to collect, as small outlay will purchase many recently used simple pieces, which will soon have rarity value. This applies particularly because hard usage and original low cost, combined with vulnerability of beech and sycamore to worm, lead to destruction of most simple pieces once they are passed serviceability. Consequently little kitchen treen has survived and the cost of earlier pieces is now unrelated to intrinsic value.

HOBS AND POT STANDS—An unusual and probably unique piece is the tilting hob (right, 34), which dates from the sixteenth or early seventeenth century. It apparently served as a stand for long-handled stew pots, when removed from the fire. By raising the wooden bracket on its ratchet, the handle of the pot lying across the bracket was lifted, so tilting the pot to facilitate ladling out the final dregs. The hob is of fruitwood and the ratchet post is finished with a carved head of Shakespeare.

The base grille shows extensive signs of burning, but it is so ingeniously constructed that any wooden member, when burnt excessively, can be removed easily. As was customary at the period, the whole piece has been constructed without glue and the base grillage is triangulated on modern engineering principles. Each wooden slat comprising the grille is secured by the tight fit of its pointed ends into "V" grooves in another member. The height is 12½ in., length 18 in. and width 10 in.

The Victorian kettle or teapot stand (front, 38) is walnut, carved with ivy leaves.

POTS, BOWLS, DISHES, PLATTERS AND SPOONS—The large wooden pot (34) is 16 in. high by 7¾ in. diameter and is turned from a solid block. It has considerable age and good colour. I consider it is not less than 200 years old, probably much older. Made of some soft, porous wood and, therefore, unsuitable for holding liquids or acting as a churn and being unusually large and awkward to carry, it was possibly intended as a standing container for grain or as a measure. This last belief is strengthened by my recent discovery of another similar vessel of smaller size. Both came from Sussex.

The beechwood bowl with handle cut from the solid and the skimmer spoon of the same wood are types commonly used until 50 or 100 years ago; another skimmer spoon is in PLATE 35.

The large sycamore bowl (left, 34), 18 in. in diameter, was for many centuries a universal type in the kitchen for mixing, in the dairy for milk and at table for serving stews.

An interesting object sometimes to be found is an oblong, shallow wooden dish about 20 in. by 15 in., resembling a butcher's tray without the spikes. This was a dish for salting meat. Small bowls, platters, trenchers and dishes (3) were also used in the kitchen.

In front of PLATE 36 are a serrated butter slice and a simple spoon. Standing at the back is a large hook-handled ladle used in England for ladling out eggs or broth and in Scotland, where it is called a kale spoon, for ladling porridge.

STEAK BEATER, CABBAGE PRESSERS, POTATO MASHERS AND ROLLING PINS—All these have now tended to change their material, but not form. The eighteenth- or early nineteenth-century potato masher and rolling pin (34) are both good, heavy implements of boxwood made, as was customary, *en suite*. Another interesting pair, with loose rings turned from the solid, are in PLATE 35. Rolling pins with ribbed and knobbed surfaces were used largely in Wales for crushing oatcakes to make "brewis", a favourite food on Welsh farms.

The mushroom-headed cabbage presser (34) and the serrated headed steak beater (left, 35) are beech.

SPICE BOXES—Wooden spice boxes in many shapes were a feature in old English kitchens. An unusual eighteenth-century turned mahogany spice box, with radiating divisions, mounted on foot and stem, is right of PLATE 35. A circular box, with radiating divisions and nutmeg compartment and grater in the centre, was common in japanned iron 50 to 100 years ago, but the treen specimen, open in PLATE 36, is rare. A small nutmeg grater box with handle is further to the right. The circular birch column boxes (left, 37) found a place on many mantelshelves in south-east England a century ago; they were particularly a Sussex speciality. The compartments, labelled with transfers, vary from two to six; the boxes interscrew. A four-compartment box is shown with sections disconnected.

SALT BOXES—Different districts used different types. That left of PLATE 38 has been popular, with and without drawer, in farmhouses certainly since the seventeenth century. Its oak construction and ornamental appearance were ideal for kitchen-living rooms. A deeper box, of similar type but tapering towards the bottom, was used for knives and forks and was sometimes made *en suite*. Salt boxes and cutlery boxes are sometimes confused.

The alternate beech and sycamore staved box (left, 37) is well finished and moulded after assembly; it is eighteenth or early nineteenth century, probably Scottish. A lighter and cheaper variant, without the cross turning, was made in England until the end of the nineteenth century.

DRY STORE BARRELS, SCOOPS AND MEASURES—The flour barrel (centre, 37) is a pattern which remained unchanged from seventeenth to mid-nineteenth century. It has a sliding gate action bolt and is made from steamed oak. The two flour scoops nearby are beech.

The set of three kitchen measures (left, 36) are of cane. Advantage has been taken of the cane structure to use the natural cross membranes for the bottoms of all three receptacles and the lid of the largest, seen standing in front. Other dry measures are in PLATE 67. The dry store barrel, right of the shelf, is Portuguese and is made from cork, a particularly suitable material as a cork lid fitted into a cork cylinder creates an almost airtight fit, whilst the material has remarkable resistance to heat and damp. Cork, a recurrent crop, is obtained from the bark of the cork oak, which grow to perfection in Portugal. After reaching maturity, trees are stripped of bark approximately every ten years, care being taken not to damage the cambium or wood-forming layer, which lies just below the bark.

36 Strainer bowl, funnels, Welsh spoons and rack, egg timer, kale spoon and cork barrel. *Below*, spice boxes, strainer, butter slicer and spoon and four types of lemon squeezers

37 Salt and spice boxes, flour barrel, gingerbread moulds and strainer. *In front*, flour scoops, egg timer, pastry and bread stamps and coffee grinders

38   Salt box, spoon rack and cutlery cabinet, chopping board, egg timer,
drop weight mouse trap, hob and strainer

39   Different types of coffee and spice grinders, a biscuit stamp and sugar tongs

MINCERS—Mincers were made in various forms, some of them real Heath Robinson contraptions. The sturdy fruitwood specimen (35) is a late eighteenth- or early nineteenth-century model.

SPICE AND COFFEE GRINDERS—Though perhaps not strictly kitchen treen, grinders come into this chapter as appliances used in the preparation of spices, etc. There is some doubt whether coffee was introduced into England in 1650 or 1657, but certain it is that coffee-houses were so popular soon after the Restoration that Charles II made vain efforts to repress them as harbouring treasonable characters.

There is no difference between a large spice mill and a coffee grinder. Doubtless the one machine, varying in outward form at different periods, has served both purposes. Coffee beans until comparatively recently were prepared in some country places by crushing with pestle and mortar.

The earliest mill in PLATE 39 is the incomplete engine-turned lignum vitæ one on the extreme right, which may have been intended for spice and must be almost contemporary with the introduction of coffee. Nos. 1, 2 and 3 from the left are also of lignum vitæ and are 7 to 8 in. high, of the cylindrical type popular at the end of the seventeenth century; their handles fold inside them and their bases form measures for the day's supply and receptacles for the newly ground beans or spice. The fourth is mid-eighteenth century and, instead of the usual metal funnel, both box and funnel are mahogany; in this type of grinder the ground coffee falls into a drawer in the base. The fifth is beech, with drawer inlaid with brass and a brass funnel. It is probably Italian, late seventeenth or early eighteenth century.

Of the two grinders in PLATE 37, the cylindrical one on the left is lignum vitæ, late seventeenth century, and comes from Hurstmonceux Castle. That on the right is an eighteenth-century, mahogany box type, with drawer and pewter funnel. The finest quality and most interesting grinder in my collection is the specimen, probably Dutch, in PLATE 135.

LEMON SQUEEZERS—The date when lemons were introduced to England is unknown, but they are mentioned in a rare sixteenth-century sheet of woodcuts of London Cries in the British Museum. No. 3, the "Orange Woman", has the following cry:

> *"Fine Savil oranges, fine lemmons, fine;*
> *Round, sound, and tender, inside and rine,*
> *One pin's prick their vertue show:*
> *They've liquor by their weight, you may know."*

Wooden lemon squeezers were made in several forms, but invariably of close-grained hardwoods. The nutcracker type (one from right, 35), is an unusual seventeenth-century variety, made from lignum vitæ, with an oval hollow in each half to hold the lemon. A simpler variant of this pattern is standing in PLATE 36. One of the best made eighteenth-century types was the boxwood urn-shaped press with screw action to eject the juice of the squeezed lemon from the spout. One of this type is shown lying horizontally (right, 35); another is standing in PLATE 36.

The lever and frame type implement (right, 36) is a country-made piece. Its handle is oak, the frame mahogany and the "button", which presses against the inside of the half lemon, is boxwood. The eighteenth-century mahogany example in front of it employs a different principle, its oval, flanged head being used with a turning movement to scoop out a half lemon. It is interesting that some of the latest plastic models have reverted to this design.

STRAINERS—Wooden strainers followed all the simpler metal forms. A rare strainer bowl is at the back left of PLATE 36 and a 15-in. long two-handled sycamore strainer is in front. Though quite modern in form, both were made in the eighteenth century.

FUNNELS—Funnels of sycamore, once the commonest variety, are becoming rare. Five are in PLATE 36. Although all their curves differ, they follow a general form which, by analogy with pewter, is late eighteenth or early nineteenth century. The two with "bulbs" below their large curves contain ledges to seat strainers.

SPOON RACKS—These were formerly a feature of every kitchen and took many forms, but in general, eighteenth- and nineteenth-century English country-made pieces followed the lines of the oak rack (38), although some had neither cutlery box nor drawer beneath. Seventeenth-century racks are usually shallower, simple backboards with pierced, not notched, ledges for spoon handles.

The Welsh favoured the "step" type oak rack, shown in PLATE 36, with typical Welsh sycamore spoons. Note the love token fret cut.

MOULDS—It would be interesting to know when the idea first occurred of carving wood to show in reverse the design which it was desired to impart to a moulded product. In Part 5, PLATE 51 and PLATE 52, are dairy moulds going back 250 years and in PLATE 37 are gingerbread moulds, some of which are older still.

Gingerbread moulds were known as "fairings" because the gold spangled gingerbread figures of legend and fairy tale moulded in them were sold at fairs. St. Bartholomew's, the most famous fair, was held annually at Smithfield, from 1123 until 1850, by which time only gingerbread stalls remained.

A popular subject in gingerbread was the horn book (see Part 7), but even after primers took its place, gingerbread alphabets persisted, for we find in *Poems to a Bard at Bromsgrove* (J. Crane—1835):

> "*The bakers to increase their trade*
> *Made Alphabets of gingerbread*
> *That folks might swallow what they read*
> *All the letters were digested*
> *Hateful ignorance detested.*"

It is almost impossible to date the Punch and Judy mould in PLATE 37, but the chestnut specimen next to it with the three figures on it is early eighteenth century. On the back it contains six more moulds, devoted to figures and scenes from the Lord Mayor's show, including the Lord Mayor's barge. The small walnut mould on the right, with a figure riding a goat, is seventeenth century. The circular mould next to it is a very old Coptic Communion bread stamp. The sycamore wheel in the centre front was used for marking designs on pastry. Similar wheels were also used for imprinting a pattern round butter pats. The beech biscuit roller (front, 39) is for stamping York Wine Union biscuits.

Some kitchen treen of North-West Europe is discussed and illustrated in Part 16.

MISCELLANEOUS—The heavy beech chopping board (right, 38), with a scooped out hollow in the middle, is unusual. The egg timer on the left and the two other patterns central in PLATE 36, may soon be joined in museums by all their brethren if dried eggs persist. The nineteenth-century wooden sugar tongs (front, 39) are Welsh love tokens, with donors' names and dates inserted in their "windows". The very old jug carved from the solid (36) is specially made for a left-handed pourer. The inclusion of the mouse trap in PLATE 38 need not cast aspersions on cooks past or present! It is there because it was the only picture into which it would fit when I was having photographs taken in the museum of my friend, the Rev. C. J. Sharp. It is described in the appropriate place in Part 14.

*   *   *

COLLECTORS NOTES

Kitchen treen is well represented in many museums including the Tolson Memorial Museum, Huddersfield, Colchester, Brighton, Hove, Worthing, York, Cardiff, Norwich and the Rev. C. J Sharp's Museum, Shepreth. Hall-i'-th'-Wood Folk Museum shows kitchen treen against its correct background. Counterparts from North-West Europe are at Haslemere Museum, Surrey.

Anne of Cleves House, Lewes, has a salting tub, Hertfordshire County Museum, St. Albans, has some fine gingerbread moulds, and Cheltenham Museum a large eighteenth-century ginger-bread mould used at Tewkesbury Fair. Dough bins, too large to class as treen, are in many of the above museums; in the private collection of Commander F. Hart, R.N. (Retd.), at Chipping Campden, are two interesting early specimens, which have curved tops which turn over and form kneading troughs.

Mr. and Mrs. J. F. Parker's private Folk Museum at Tickenhill Manor, Bewdley, has a consider-able amount of kitchen treen, including lemon squeezers, steak beaters, rolling pins, flour scoops, spice boxes, knife cleaning machines, etc.

Other items for collectors, not illustrated in this chapter, but well represented about the country, are "oven peels"—long, flat, sharp ended wooden spades for removing bread from ovens—and their shorter brothers, the oatcake slices or cake boards, toasters, tripod stools, some-times of wood, with adjustable horizontal iron forks—and boxwood corkscrews, which are rare.

PART FOUR

LOVE TOKENS, SPOONS, LADLES, KNIVES AND FORKS

THE reason why love tokens and eating implements are grouped here is because wooden spoons were formerly the most popular love tokens among sailors and rustics.

LOVE TOKENS—Other love gifts described in this book show how widespread was the custom formerly of giving wooden articles, made and appropriately ornamented by the donors to denote affection. Moreover, the custom covered practically the whole range of domestic woodware—not merely treen: were the man sufficiently skilled, he might make and adorn with appropriate love emblems all or any of the furniture for the future home. I think, nevertheless, that there was a division in this custom and that miscellaneous articles carved with hearts often represent the man's work between bethrothal and marriage or are wedding anniversary or birthday gifts, whereas there were formerly certain wooden "Valentines"—recognised preludes to courtship, acceptance of which by the recipient signified some measure of approval of the giver.

The love spoon, which at one time represented the almost universal language of Welsh rustic courtship, was used to a lesser extent in many European countries, particularly Scandinavia, where distaffs attained popularity for the same purpose. Love spoons were much more a Welsh than English custom, though "spooning", derived from the custom, has passed into the English language. At various times and in different parts of the country, gift spoons were substituted by stay busks and the more practical knitting sheaths and lace bobbins.

These tokens were PRELUDES to courtship, not equivalents of engagement rings, and they were offered by the man as a sign that courtship was desired; consequently, a village belle, were she a coquette, might accept a spoon from divers would-be suitors.

When the custom originated is unknown, but most existing love spoons are eighteenth- and nineteenth-century work. Some simple ones were undoubtedly intended for practical use, but many were too elaborate to be more than symbolic. The actual symbolism, as applied to courting, seems to have originated in spoons of similar size fitting close to each other. In Trotter's *Distressed Seamen* (1789), the sentence occurs "they are stowed sponways and so closely locked in one another's arms that it is difficult to move".

The whole of PLATE 40, PLATE 41, PLATE 42 and part of PLATE 43 are devoted to love spoons, without by any means exhausting the fertility of imagination displayed in their creation. First (left, 40), 10 in. long, has the handle amusingly carved to represent a pair of spectacles. The second, 9¼ in. long, from Glamorgan, is inscribed "M.I. 1727". The third, 10 in. long, is a fine early nineteenth-century creation; it includes four lanterns with loose balls carved from the solid and is inscribed "A. PHS." The fourth, with loose ring and revolving hook let into the lantern, is interesting because of its heart-shaped bowl. The modern example (centre top) consists of a beautiful pair of sycamore love spoons on heart-shaped stand. Dated 1937 and made by D. Lewis, Ffostrasol, Cardiganshire, for the Llangeithe Eisteddfod 1937, it won first prize. An "Eisteddfod" is a yearly festival of music, poetry, and drama and occasionally arts and crafts.

The left spoon (41), cut from one piece of wood 12 by 7 in., is inlaid in small squares with red sealing wax and must have taken many hours of some sailor's time. According to some authorities, the large central spoon signifies desire for a large family.

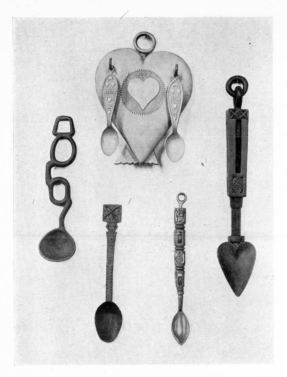

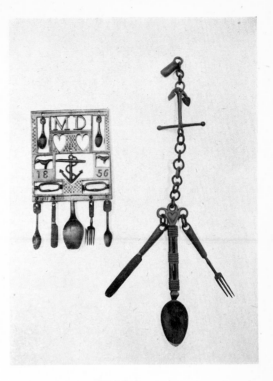

40 Welsh love spoons

41 Welsh love spoons

42 Welsh love spoons

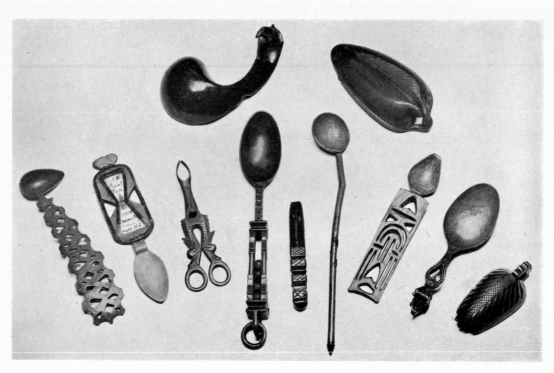

43   Welsh love spoons, sugar tongs, apple and other scoops

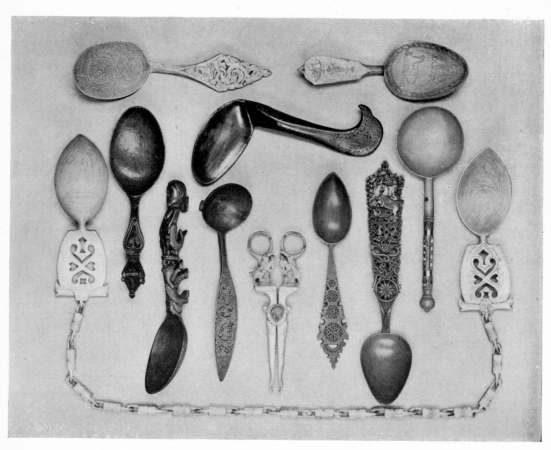

44   Ornamental spoons, mainly from North-West Europe

The equally original knife, fork and spoon on an anchored chain (right) is also a sailor's gift. The top terminates in a whistle and is carved from one piece of wood 26 in. long.

The outsize sycamore spoon (bottom, 42) is 27 in. long. Carved with the name "Margaret Thomas" in a border, it has a hook under the handle, carved from the solid. The next above is unusual, with its four windows displaying textiles; the carving is inlaid with red and black sealing wax. Two spoon bowls sprouting from one handle were supposed to mean "We two are one". The large sycamore double spoon, dated 1865, says this, but being carved with hearts it also says "I love you" and the wheels signify "I will work for you"—quite a long message in wood. Spade-handled spoons probably also signify working for the beloved. Keys, keyholes or miniature houses in the carving mean "My house is yours".

The small spoon on the left at the top is unusual, the handle taking the form of a hand grasping a book. The pointed thumb shows on the face and the four fingers on the reverse. The next spoon, with the broad handle pierced with hearts, has two lanterns in the stem, each containing six loose balls carved from the solid. The spoon on the right at the top of the picture is another sailor's token, cut from yew wood; its handle, carved with a fish and a sailing vessel, is connected to the bowl by a carved rope stem. The sycamore spoon (below) has a lantern with three balls in the stem and a double spade handle with a wood ring inserted. Below is a typical Welsh crooked spoon.

MISCELLANEOUS—PLATE 43 shows a varied selection of implements. The love spoon (left), with bowl at right angles to the heart and diamond pierced handle, is an unusual love spoon. Next is an amusingly crude specimen, relating in its glass window that it is "A present from Dyffryn Merioneth Shere. Maker H.R." The third, a pair of walnut sugar tongs, is Swiss. The fourth, with four loose balls in the lantern, though not specially elaborate, is an unusually well-carved Welsh love spoon of sycamore, $11\frac{1}{2}$ in. long. The fifth is a seventeenth- or early eighteenth-century country-made wooden apple scoop. These are much commoner in bone than wood. Two well-made bone specimens with walnut handles, one carved with a squirrel eating a nut and one with a crown, initials and the date 1874 are at the bottom (47). Similar implements with wider blades are cheese scoops or spitters. Number 6 is a crooked spoon with acorn knop; the shape of the handles of these spoons was designed to facilitate tipping liquid into the mouth with minimum wrist movement. I doubt whether this one is Welsh, though most crooked spoons are. An unusually carved Caernarvon crooked spoon, with bird's-head handle, is lying horizontal in PLATE 44. Number 7 in PLATE 43 is a crude Welsh love spoon and number 8 an unusually fine one, probably Scandinavian. This photograph does not do it justice, so it appears again in PLATE 44. It measures 7 in. and the gracefully curved handle is pierced through from all four sides, as is the crown-shaped terminal both above and below its central cushion. In its small area, the heart motif appears no less than fifteen times. On the back of the unusually uptilted bowl are intertwined the initials "H.S."; this rare specimen is late seventeenth or early eighteenth century.

The vessel face downwards in front right of PLATE 43 is a child's eighteenth-century pap boat; it is shown face upwards near right (48). The ladle and scoop (face downwards, top 43) are both well carved from yew wood; they are shown face up in PLATE 48. The ladle has a curious double curve, a hook on the back of the handle and a roundel and flowers on its face. The scoop, formed as a double pod, is finely carved with leaves on the back; the intertwined stems forming the handle terminate in snake heads on the face side.

Like eating and drinking bowls, the earliest spoons, ladles and dippers were fish and nut shells. Later, these were fitted into cleft twigs to act as handles and so spoons were formed. By 4000 B.C., spoons were in fairly common use in Egypt and examples in flint, wood and ivory, some elaborately carved, are in the British Museum, together with Greek and Roman metal spoons of fine workmanship.

In the Dark Ages, after the overthrow of European and Northern Asiatic civilisation by the Huns and Goths in the third to fifth centuries A.D., all traces of spoons, like most other articles of refinement, were lost and only in the fourteenth century do they begin to figure in inventories of kings and nobles as rare and valuable articles. Most fourteenth-to early seventeenth-century specimens still extant are silver or pewter, but probably the majority in use in average households were wooden and, being of little value, were scrapped when worn. The few English wooden specimens surviving from this period possess little artistic merit, but follow, in general, the form of simple metal spoons, varying in size according to requirements. Apart from salt spoons, most had fig-shaped bowls, the point of the fig at the top joining the handle and the bowl tilting upwards in a manner reminiscent of the earlier shell, inserted in a twig. In the seventeenth century, at the time of the Restoration, the bowl of the spoon, then called a "spon", tended to straighten in relation to the stem, which in wood terminated either in what was known as a slip end or in a knop. Some knops or knobs were square and others round, hexagonal, spear-head or acorn-shaped. Simultaneously, the fig-shape of the bowl became inverted, with the round at top and the point at bottom, or sometimes it became ovoid and the spoon adopted much the form and uses known to-day.

UTILITARIAN SPOONS—It is curious how the Welsh are particularly associated with wooden spoon making. Insistence on dignity of craftsmanship can be traced in Welsh life through the ages. Iorwerth C. Peate, M.A., F.S.A., writing in the *Guide to the Collection Illustrating Welsh Folk Crafts and Industries in the National Museum of Wales, Cardiff*, says:

> "The highest form of craftsmanship in every age is that which solves the problem of wedding beauty of form with usefulness, of making necessary things both functional and beautiful."

This answers perfectly those who have developed, successfully, the cult of the hideous, by claiming that because their works are functional, they are automatically beautiful. The guide referred to above gives a good description of wooden spoon and ladle making.

SPOONS OF NORTH-WEST EUROPE—Most of the spoons in PLATE 44 are from North-West Europe. The making of the pair of finely chained love spoons was no mean feat; they are carved from one block of sycamore 3 ft. long, $2\frac{1}{4}$ in. wide and, owing to the acute upward tilt of the spoon bowls, at least $1\frac{1}{2}$ in. thick.

The Russian spoon with silver filigree on the handle (first right) is described in the next section. Second right is an unusually fine boxwood example; it has a thin, sharply uptilted bowl and its handle is carved extremely delicately with a mounted St. George slaying a dragon. Also included in its intricacies are birds, flowers, foliage, snakes and a roundel, all inlaid with silver pin points. Doubt exists about its country of origin, but general opinion is Persia.

Third right is a neatly chip-carved and fretted Scandinavian spoon, with well-finished bowl. Central, the Swiss sugar tongs are amusing, but obviously intended more to demonstrate the carver's skill than for use. The handles are designed as trees with looped branches, in front of which peasants, mounted on goats, are tilting at each other. They are standing on pedestals, whose bases are inward curved and end in scrolls

46   16th and 17th century carved boxwood handles of fine quality

45   German ceremonial spoon of boxwood dated 1676

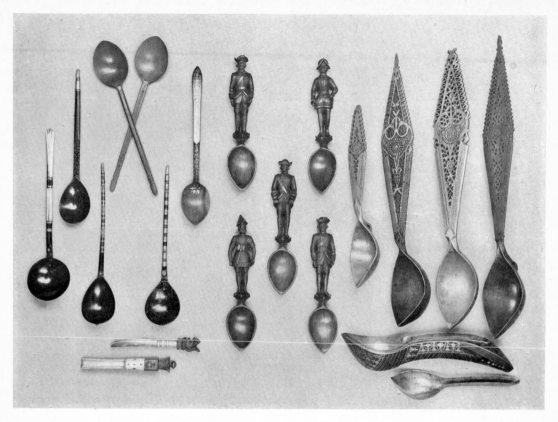

47 *Left:* Turkish spoons, apple scoops below.   *Central:* "Swiss Guard" spoons.   *Right:* Persian sherbert spoons, including a nest of six

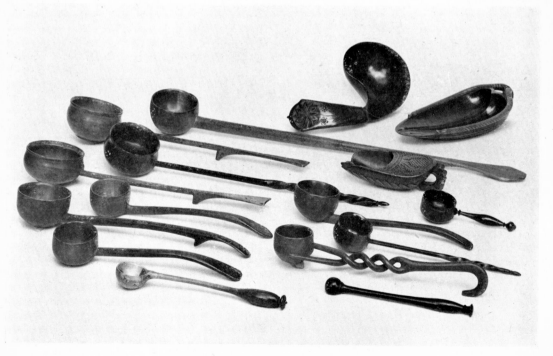

48   Miscellaneous ladles, a child's pap boat and two scoops

either side of a clown's head, which acts as pivot and whose outstretched hands form the tongs.

The Scandinavian ladle (fifth right) is well carved and graceful and has a side lip of paper thickness cut from the solid, an unusual feature in wood. Next is another Scandinavian example, most unusual and elaborate. At top of the handle a mermaid holds a shield, the base of which is bound with rope. Springing from this base a downward thrusting hand grasps an unshod cow hoof, a shod horse's hoof and a pair of high boots. I have not solved the symbolism of these very varied terminals. The two spoons at the top are typical nineteenth-century Scandinavian work and have engraved bowls and carved handles.

RITUALISTIC SPOONS—In addition to acting as love tokens and for strictly utilitarian purposes, spoons have always figured prominently in church ritual, including the Coronation ceremony. Elaborately carved boxwood spoons were given as christening presents and were used also for the chrism holy oil, for removing wafers for mass out of the ciborus, for mixing water with wine in the chalice and for transferring grains of incense from the navette to the censer. Many fifteenth-, sixteenth- and seventeenth-century ritual spoons were artistically carved all over with religious subjects.

The ceremonial spoon (right, 44), one of a pair, is Russian and of very thin boxwood, with the handle banded with fine silver filigree, inlaid with coloured enamels.

A magnificent German ceremonial spoon, dated 1676, is the subject of PLATE 45. Of boxwood, the whole of this masterpiece is carved in a length of $7\frac{3}{4}$ in. Adam and Eve embracing, form the junction of stem and bowl, and below them are the Virgin and Child. The handle terminal is carved in the form of a seated monkey. The inverted fig-shaped bowl is carved in wonderful detail, including inside a portrait and inscription in German and outside an equestrian figure of a German Elector.

PERSIAN SHERBERT SPOONS AND TURKISH SPOONS—No account of wooden spoons would be complete without mention of Persian sherbert spoons (right, 47), which are just lace work in wood. They vary from 9 in. to 16 in. in length and have 2 in. deep boat-shaped bowls of paper thickness. They are nineteenth century. A delicate nest of six eighteenth-century specimens are at the foot of the picture. The smallest is shown apart.

Left are seven examples of old Turkish spoons, formerly in the collection of the late Mrs. Neville Jackson. The handles are variously decorated with silver inlay, mother-of-pearl, amber and coral. The two at the bottom have inverted fig-shaped bowls of coconut shell, which follow early principles by being inserted in clefts in the handles. The crossed spoons are designed to nest together by means of a tongue on one handle, which engages a groove on the other.

SOUVENIR SPOONS—Silver or brass souvenir spoons, engraved or enamelled with views or crests, are common; so are crude wooden ones, but well carved wooden specimens are worth collecting. The Swiss Guard spoons of the late eighteenth or early nineteenth century (centre, 47) come under this heading.

LADLES—All the wooden ladles (48) date from the seventeenth and eighteenth centuries and most are sycamore. They vary in length from $7\frac{1}{2}$ to 17 in. and were used chiefly with wassail or punch bowls. To prevent them slipping into the bowl, they were often provided with a projecting lug under the handle or occasionally, as in the specimen with double open twist, the end of the handle was hooked. The short cordial ladle (right), with spindle-turned handle and the two ladles with twisted whalebone handles, which come from Scotland, have their handles threaded into their lignum vitæ bowls. The other ladles, which are English, have handles and bowls cut from a single piece.

KNIFE AND FORK HANDLES—Until the sixteenth century wooden spoons or the fingers conveyed food to the mouth. Forks were known in fourteenth-century England, but were only used for serving fruits and sweetmeats. They were considered effeminate and were little used for eating for the next 300 years. In the sixteenth century a large serving knife or spoon was provided at table and guests brought their own knives and forks, or more often spoons, with them. Some of these and the cases which held them were real works of art.

A rare silver-mounted, finely carved boxwood case, 8½ in. long, dated 1611, with knife and fork, is left of PLATE 46. Signed with the initials of the unknown master "W.G.W.", it is believed to be North German or Flemish. I know of five almost identical sheaths bearing this signature. One, dated 1602, is in New Place Museum, Stratford-on-Avon; two, dated respectively 1593 and 1615, are in the Debruge Dumesnil collection in Paris; one dated 1577 was in the Redpath collection and one dated 1626 in the Owen Evan-Thomas collection. The one illustrated is decorated with fine rope borders enclosing, on each of two sides, six minute carvings of biblical scenes depicting the history of the Prodigal Son and Six Works of Mercy (Matthew xxv, verses 35–36). On the side shown and also opposite are six small panels of the Apostles. The other knife and fork, with finely carved, silver-mounted boxwood handles, were no doubt also once carried in a case. The well-worn handles are deeply carved with cherub heads and figures depicting the four virtues—Faith, Hope, Charity and Justice. The silver caps are engraved with a coat of arms and the initials "K.V.B." under a crown; they are seventeenth century, possibly Bohemian. The folding penknife is the earliest folding knife I have seen. It has its original steel blade and silver mount and a richly patinated boxwood handle, carved with a dainty representation of Eve handing the apple to Adam, while the grinning serpent between their feet offers another apple in its mouth. The Tree of Knowledge or Life, against which the figures lean, is divided centrally to form a sheath for the folding blade. It is sixteenth-century Italian work of superb quality.

The knife handle to the right, another fine specimen in boxwood, shows a well-posed and draped figure of David with the sling at his left hand and the head of Goliath in his right. It is seventeenth century, Flemish.

The boxwood handle below, the most inspired carving of all, shows the Angel of the Lord restraining the right hand of Abraham, who is about to slay the bound and kneeling figure of Isaac on his left. This early seventeenth-century Flemish piece shows vivid imagination and great skill.

The superb quality 12 in. long boxwood handle (extreme right) is not a knife handle. It may have been intended for a hand "pointer" or a censer for church use. The details of execution equal the technical mastery of design. The top is finely carved with four figures of the virtues—Faith, Hope, Charity and Justice—surmounted by cherub heads and a lion couchant. The tapering stem is magnificently carved with a coat of arms and nine minute scenes representing the Judgment of Solomon, Joseph and his Brethren and Salome with the head of John the Baptist. It is late sixteenth century.

*   *   *

COLLECTORS NOTES

The National Museum of Wales, Cardiff, and the Rev. C. J. Sharp's Museum, Shepreth, both have outstanding collections of Welsh love spoons. Several small museums in Wales have good specimens. Examples of plain wooden spoons are in County Museums throughout the British Isles.

For fine art examples of spoons and knife and fork handles in boxwood, the British Museum, the Wallace Collection and the Victoria and Albert Museum cannot be surpassed. The latter museum also possesses superb specimens of Persian sherbert spoons. The British Museum, Department of Egyptology, has specimens of wooden spoons dating back thousands of years.

49 Two churns, a butter pan and a yoke

50 A flail, a fine James I chessel and two butter scoops

51 A cheese stand, four cheese moulds, a piggin and five butter prints

52   A swinging churn, lidded cheese mould, butter scales, whisk, butter prints and piggin

53   Piggin "laced" with ash bands and Welsh butter prints

PART FIVE

ON THE FARM

FARM treen, particularly dairy utensils, have considerable homely charm when displayed suitably, as in simply furnished oak-beamed cottages. During the past 150 years mechanised methods of farming have outmoded much farm treen and larger wooden apparatus. The Industrial Revolution is usually ascribed to James Watt and his steam engine of 1765, but Jethro Tull of Basildon, Berks (1674–1741) revolutionised farming with his four-coultered plough and seed drill in 1733, and by making two pounds of seed, sown in drills, produce the same crop as nine or ten pounds sown broadcast, he literally laid the seed which nearly trebled the population in the eighteenth century and so provided the workers required for mechanised industry.

Until Tull's day, farms produced barely enough for the existing population; a bad harvest meant death for many, but Tull's methods, though converting the larger wooden apparatus into the first agricultural machines, left the smaller dairy utensils and field implements untouched and there were few alterations before about 1880. Until change in farming methods superseded a device, it continued correct for its unchanging purpose and was unaffected by fashion's vagaries. Consequently, though it is easy to see whether a piece is new or old, it is usually impossible to say how old.

Most extant farm treen is eighteenth and nineteenth century. Hard use, combined with low intrinsic value and the particular vulnerability to worm of most of the woods employed, make it unlikely that collectors will find anything antedating 1700. It is probable also that, apart from sycamore, beech, ash, elm and chestnut being woods prone to attack, they are made more delectable to worm because of their impregnation with fats, both in dairy and kitchen.

DAIRY TREEN—In large eighteenth- and most nineteenth-century dairies, butter was made in churns revolved by means of cogged wheels, actuated by one (actual) horse-power. In smaller dairies, churns similar to PLATE 49, box-churns, or over-end churns with side handles were hand operated. These, together with the butter pan, milkmaid's beech yoke, shown in the same picture, and the familiar three-legged stool were the largest average dairy woodware. In conjunction with the yoke, coopered wood buckets were used in dairy and on the "round", which was heralded by the cry "Milk, maids below", later shortened to "Milk below", which has now reached the stage of "Milko" or sometimes "Miaow".

Another coopered vessel largely employed was the milk piggin (left, 51). Apart from these, practically all dairy treen was provided by the turner, who made bowls, cheese vats or moulds, butter prints, scales and milk skimmers, saucer-shaped vessels which, in Wales particularly, were "turned" to almost transparent thinness at the rim and were used without a handle.

In PLATE 52 the butter scales are beech and the swinging churn on the left is sycamore. Note the love token carving on the whisk. The piggin-type staved vessel (right), narrower at top than base, was probably a cream measure. The two butter moulds or prints, of which the larger gives the impress of a cow and the smaller that of a cock, are of the ejector pattern, still used, which act as butter measures. In front of PLATE 51 are three more sycamore moulds. The smallest is plain, the second strawberry pattern and the one side-on gives a shell impress. The circular stamp imprints three acorns and the two-piece beech mould, which creates a Crown in butter, is the Royal Mould of 1820 from St. James's Palace.

The four cheese vats of elm, in the same photograph, vary in diameter from $5\frac{1}{2}$ to 8 in. They are easily distinguishable from ordinary bowls by their straight sides and weep holes near the edges, which vary from four to eight. On the extreme left the heavy chestnut circle, 14 in. in diameter, has no weep holes, being a cheese stand, not a vat. It formerly belonged to the Duke of Montrose of Buchanan Castle. In PLATE 52, next to the swinging churn on the left, is a lidded cheese mould. For making large cheeses, until the late eighteenth century at least, primitive large weighted box-type presses with windlasses were used to extract the last drops of whey from the curd.

All the butter prints (53) are Welsh; the canoe-shaped ones, with heart motifs, both approximately 8 in. long, are of a form which I have not found outside Wales. The $8\frac{1}{4}$ in. dumbell-shaped print is unusual and stamps four different designs, each of different diameter. The centre front print, $11\frac{1}{2}$ in. long, imparts two designs in different sizes. In contrast to the naturalistic carved reliefs of English prints, the Welsh counterparts are characterised by geometrical designs, largely based on the roundel and closely resembling some of the treen illustrated in Part 16. The $5\frac{3}{4}$ in. milk piggin (back of photograph) is posed to show the skilled manner of lacing the ash bands.

The Royal cheese print (50), or chessel to give it its correct name, is "Royal" in every sense, being $18\frac{1}{2}$ in. in diameter, cut from a single piece of chestnut. The "College of Arms" cannot date it with certainty, but consider it was probably made prior to the Union of 1707. When bought, its use seemed long forgotten under multitudinous layers of paint, applied by successive misguided decorators, who had treated it as a heraldic device, ignoring the fact that the coat of arms appeared in reverse. It had received at least eight coats of paint since ending its active career and its deepest depression was less than mine after the first day's "stripping". It presented a formidable task; it had been black, yellow, red, polychrome, cream, white and finally what older readers would recognise as "a rich shade of Victorian hip-bath oak graining". It has amply repaid the work of stripping and if the long dead craftsman who carved it could see it now, he would rejoice at its mellow colour and patina and the restored clarity and depth of the lines which he created.

The scoops to right and left of the chessel were used to scoop butter out of the churn and the handle of that on the left can be used as a "print".

AGRICULTURAL TREEN—Old wooden agricultural implements are interesting but hardly decorative. Until last century, the form of most had not changed since the days of the Pharaohs who, in carving and painting, are often depicted seated in judgment, holding their symbolic crook and flail. Flails of the type in PLATE 50 were at one time universally used for threshing corn, beans and peas. The implement consists of two strong sticks, called the hand staff and the swipple or souple. They are bound together by leather thongs and the handstaff is fitted with an iron pin and band and a loose wooden socket, so that the swipple can revolve as it swings. Ash was the wood used most commonly. It forms the handstaff of the example illustrated; the swipple is of thorn.

Grain shovels, larger editions of a child's spade, with a large concave blade, were and still are used in granaries. Wooden hay rakes were the principal implements used in haymaking until a hundred years ago and they are still made by hand and occasionally used in Hampshire. Wooden hayforks were not only made, they were grown. In England it was usual to select a tree branch which forked naturally into two prongs and then peg a third prong, but in Southern France there existed a thriving industry in training and growing natural three-prong forks. The wood of the Micocoulier, a member of the elm family, was used and by careful pollarding, trees were induced to shoot out prongs where required.

In various parts of England, wooden thatching needles were used until about 100 years ago. They were about 2 ft. long and 1 in. in diameter, with a ¾ in. eye. Before the use of yarn, flexible stems of blackberry and wild clematis were used to tie the first coat of the thatch to the rafters. A long box, with one end open, called a wooden glove, was used for feeding gorse into gorse mills.

Until about 1870, sickles with teeth were in general use; now they are rare. Rattles of the "police" type (115) were also used for scaring rooks.

*   *   *

COLLECTORS NOTES

Most of our County Museums possess selections of the treen illustrated and described in this chapter. Cardiff and Bristol are particularly noteworthy as, in addition to real treen, they also show such larger devices and machines as farm tumbrils, various ploughs, dog and horse churns, heavy cheese presses, etc. The place to study the evolution of agricultural machines is the Science Museum, South Kensington, which has original models of reaping machines, horse churns, etc. Luton Museum has a comprehensive collection of the smaller agricultural devices. The natural grown hay forks described are in Museum No. 1, Royal Botanic Gardens, Kew.

Wooden box churns are at the "Georgian House", Bristol, one of the best furnished period houses in the country. Brighton Museum and the Bucks County Museum, Aylesbury, have much of interest.

Among unusual pieces, Cardiff has a wooden glove for gorse feeding, grease boxes used for sharpening agricultural implements and a primitive but effective hay and straw carrier.

Hereford Museum and Rye and District Museum both specialise in old agricultural implements. Bradford, Tolson Memorial Museum, Huddersfield, Cheltenham and Worthing Museums have a good collection of agricultural implements and devices; the latter museum displays a hop stirrer and yeast chutes.

Hall-i'-th'-Wood Folk Museum, Bolton, shows a dairy, well equipped with old treen, as well as many interesting obsolete farming implements. Bishop Hooper's Lodgings, now Gloucester's Folk Museum, a timber framed building in which Bishop Hooper was lodged the night before being burned at the stake, has numerous examples of dairy and agricultural treen.

In the Isle of Man butter prints apparently were formerly made and given for love tokens, for in the Manx Museum, Douglas, are several prints with carved hearts in the design. Several dairy piggins, called "goggans" by the Manxmen, are displayed in the Museum. In addition to dairy use, they were utilised for porridge, like the Scottish equivalent, the "luggie", referred to in Part 2. Other dairy treen at Douglas includes cheese presses and wooden lidded butter bowls, known as "Mealley-begs", used by Manx fishermen on fishing expeditions and by shepherds when they went up to the hills in summer.

Farm and dairy treen is well represented in Belfast Municipal Museum.

PART SIX

TOBACCO

WOOD'S influence on the tobacco habit is as important as on drinking. Quite apart from specialised treen, the mind's eye automatically conjures up the old-fashioned tobacconist's shop with wood predominant. The small paned door, with welcoming light shining out, is framed in a doorway with fluted pilasters and canopy surmounted by the tobacconist's sign—a carved wooden Red Indian smoking his pipe or a kilted Scot with his ram's horn snuff mull, the latter denoting that Scotch snuff is sold. To left and right, the well proportioned bow windows project invitingly over their panelled stallboards.

Inside there is more wood than tobacco. The polished oak floor supports counter, shelving and stools of warm mahogany or oak; the mellow panelling provides a background to hogsheads, small barrels, cedar cabinets and cigar boxes. Display cases enshrine fine quality wooden tobacco and snuff boxes, rasps, pipes, pipe cases and pipe stoppers.

Without wood, tobacco might never have been used in Europe either for snuff or smoking. A brief glance into history will confirm this. Colombus, the first known European to report on tobacco, observed smoking on his first voyage to the Bahamas and West Indies in 1492 and snuff taking on his second voyage, 1494–96. In 1502 the Spaniards reported that the weed had been chewed in South America from time immemorial and was considered "good medicine".

The natives of Central America inhaled smoke from dry leaves of tobacco by means of Y-shaped canes, the double end of which they inserted in the nostrils, holding the other end over the burning leaves. This early pipe, not its contents, was called "tabaco". The custom on many West Indian Islands was to roll tobacco into a kind of cigar.

Francisco Hernandez, a Spanish physician, introduced the plant to Spain in 1559, in which year Jean Nicot, French Ambassador to Portugal, in sending seeds of the plant to Catherine de Medici, Queen of France, gave his name to nicotine. Tobacco grown in North America is reported to have been introduced into England in 1565 by Sir John Hawkins. Certainly Ralph Lane, Governor of Virginia, brought some home in 1586 and presented it to Sir Walter Raleigh, who smoked it and had a bucket of water thrown over him by his alarmed servant. The episode apparently did not damp Raleigh's ardour for, to meet his needs, he cultivated the plant in Ireland during 1587 and subsequent years.

Smoking and snuffing have alternated in popularity several times since and have suffered considerable vicissitudes. In the seventeenth century Church and State in various parts of Europe combined to ban tobacco. Innocent XII excommunicated those who took snuff or tobacco in St. Peter's, Rome. At Bern prohibition of tobacco was incorporated in the Ten Commandments. In Russia the penalty for men and women was public knouting, or amputation of the nose, whilst in Turkey death was the punishment. James I wrote a *Counterblast to Tobacco* (1604) in which he complained of nobles and gentry spending several hundred pounds per annum on tobacco. He concluded "Smoking is a custom loathsome to the eye, hateful to the nose, harmful to the brain, dangerous to the lungs, and in the black stinking fume thereof resembling the horrible stygian smoke of the pit that is bottomless". In further efforts to discourage tobacco, James raised the duty from 2d. to 6s. 10d. per lb.

Persecution, as usual, only strengthened faith and by 1614 there was upwards of 7,000 shops selling tobacco in and near London. Later in the seventeenth century tobacco, both as snuff and for smoking, was prescribed by doctors for its disinfecting properties

54 "Quality" snuff rasps and snuff boxes. Mainly French

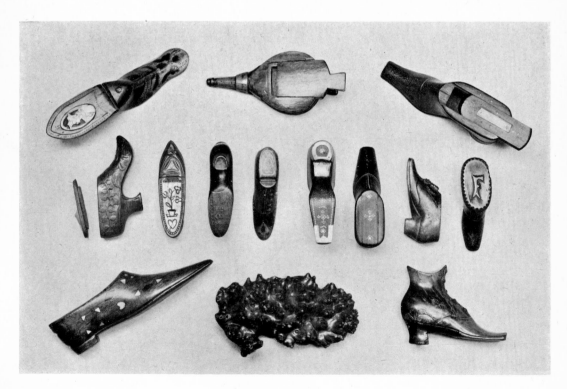

55 Shoe, bellows and burr snuff boxes

56　Miscellaneous snuff boxes

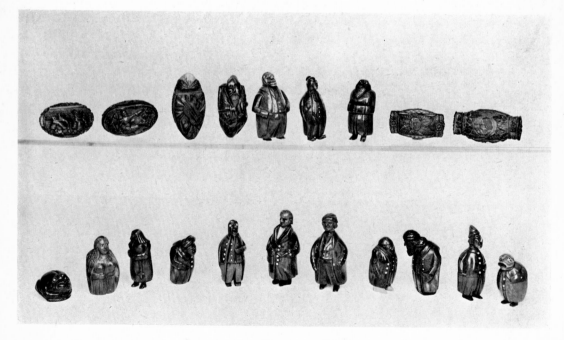

57　Coquilla nut snuff boxes

and was even used in English churches as incense. The plague of 1665 gave the habit further impetus, smokers being considered immune and even children being taught to smoke. It is related that a certain Etonian was whipped for not smoking when so instructed by his master. Celia Fiennes found the practice most distasteful for she complains that at St. Austell in 1698 ". . . both men women and children have all their pipes of tobacco in their mouths and soe sit round the fire smoking, it was not delightfull to me . . ." (*Journeys of Celia Fiennes*). Recently, the usual form of persecution for smokers has been an ever increasing rate of taxation.

By 1700 consumption had reached 2 lb. per head per annum of the entire population of Britain, smoking among women and children being then very prevalent. Soon after, smoking suffered a decline among the gentry and died out almost entirely among women and children. In the eighteenth-century world of fashion, snuff boxes ousted tobacco boxes, though pipe smoking continued, chiefly among the lower classes. That it was not confined entirely to the latter is disclosed by two entries in Parson Woodforde's diary: in 1793 he bought a "groce (gross) of pipes for 3/–" and in 1794 "$\frac{1}{4}$ lb. of pigtail tobacco for 8d." The pound certainly went much further then! Early in the nineteenth century, the duty on cigars and cheroots was reduced and smoking resumed popularity. By 1850, consumption averaged 1 lb. per head per annum of the population, which was not very high, but not surprising considering no "decent" women of the Victorian era could be seen smoking and men of fashion only indulged out of doors, in secret, or in the stables or gun room. Between 1850 and 1870, man proving incurable, the Victorians re-introduced smoking rooms, which, as Celia Fiennes' diary shows, were popular in 1685–96. Here Victorian men could retire but, if properly trained, they first removed their jackets and donned smoking jackets and caps to prevent their hair and clothing becoming contaminated. In 1868, legislation provided that railways should set apart certain carriages for smokers; times change and now "certain carriages" are set apart for non-smokers!

Consequent upon their contact with the Turks, the armies engaged in the Crimean war brought back to Western Europe a liking for cigarettes, which have steadily risen in popularity until now, with women smoking nearly as much as men, consumption averages per annum 4 lb. per head of our population.

Unlike England, where tobacco was first used for smoking, in France the first main use was as snuff, which was prescribed as strongly there by the medical profession as smoking in England a century later. In honour of Catherine de Medici, tobacco became known as the "Queen's Herb" and enjoyed great popularity as a cure for one of the periodic plagues of that time, characterised by a nasal affection which was greatly relieved by sniffing powdered tobacco.

SNUFF RASPS AND BOXES—Tobacco "rasps" or "rapes", called "rappoirs" in France, were invented to enable snuff addicts to prepare their own fresh snuff by grating into powder tightly rolled tobacco bundles or "carottes" which, prior to purchase in bulk, had been dipped in spiced oils. The French called the resultant powder "tabac râpé" or "tabac en poudre" and in England snuff was formerly called rapee. Snuff, when first introduced, was a great luxury and consequently the rappoir had to be worthy of the commodity and its user.

Most fine rappoirs were of French, Italian, Flemish or German origin and they were made of silver, tortoiseshell, ivory and wood; PLATE 54 shows a selection of fine quality treen specimens. Except for the giant rasp (top), all are pocket size, but the two narrow ones have exposed steel graters at the back, so unless carried in cases, they would speedily have torn a pocket to ribbons.

The outsize boxwood rasp is finely carved and the coat of arms and border are further embellished with brass piqué. In this process, holes are pierced with a heated instrument, fine silver or brass wires then inserted, fused into position by heat and cut off flush. This eighteenth-century rasp is 14 in. long, probably made for an Austrian Archduke.

The 8 in. boxwood rasp (left), with sliding protective shutter, was formerly in the Drane collection; it has silver piqué lines around panels carved in floral scrolls. Central in the front panel is an arrow-pierced heart and the initials "I.S."; central in the back panel appears the inscription "1775 RECHD V BASCHN". The snuff was poured out through the spout. The exquisitely carved centre rasp, $6\frac{1}{4}$ in. long, also boxwood, is one of the earliest I have seen. It is seventeenth century, French. The pivoted front shutter, carved with delicate floral sprays above a cartouche, has as central motif a fountain spraying the roots of a tree and the inscription "IE LARROSE DE BON EAU". The carving on the back includes a bird standing on the summit of a flower-grown mound.

The 8 in. long boxwood rasp (bottom) is a very fine seventeenth-century French one. Formerly in the Heseltine collection, it is carved with conventional foliage, a cupid head and coat of arms. The walnut rasp (extreme right), rather crudely carved, is seventeenth century, Italian. The bird in the circle at the top is enclosed in a border carved with the name "Joseph Lanti" (not "Sante", as described in Owen Evan-Thomas' book). The rappoirs immediately left and right of the centre are both seventeenth- or eighteenth-century Eastern Mediterranean and each is inlaid with mother-of-pearl and brass piqué. They are also love tokens; that on the left, formerly in the Owen Evan-Thomas collection, has pearl heart motifs on the back. The one on the right came from the Hilton Price collection.

Snuff, called "sneesh" in Scotland and "snisin" in Wales, only became popular in the British Isles late in the seventeenth century. In the early eighteenth century, a large cargo of prepared snuff was captured off the Spanish coast, brought to England and distributed widely. Its sudden arrival on such a large scale led to a great demand for snuff boxes and, by drawing attention to the saving of labour of ready prepared snuff, it led to commercial manufacture and sounded the death knell of the pocket rasp in England. Consequently, snuff rasps of English origin are rare and usually crude.

A seventeenth- or eighteenth-century English or probably Welsh grater (for it came from a remote part of Wales) is the vessel resembling a double mortar (right of shelf, 59). The grater forms the base of the upper bowl; the lower portion, which is detachable, forms the receptacle for the ground snuff. It was probably used in a public house or shop, for the wholesale preparation of snuff from "carottes". Somewhat similar graters or mortars were used in conjunction with pestles for grinding peppercorns.

Occasionally rasps were combined in snuff boxes; slightly more often snuff boxes were included in rasps—of the latter I have several examples. Large circular snuff boxes, about 6 in. in diameter, like the "curl" mahogany example (right bottom, 59) behind the engine-turned cigarette stand, were intended originally for patrons of public houses. Publicans also used extra large rasps and ground fresh leaves daily for their customers to have a free pinch from the box on the counter. This custom probably originated the proverb "that only he was a true man who could serve a friend with a pinch".

Snuff boxes, even more frequently than rappoirs, were conceived as works of art and executed by the greatest craftsmen of the day in tortoiseshell, papier mâché and wood. They were jewelled, engraved, carved, inlaid and painted with miniatures. Those of treen are more humble and much less valuable, although many are artistic and beautifully finished.

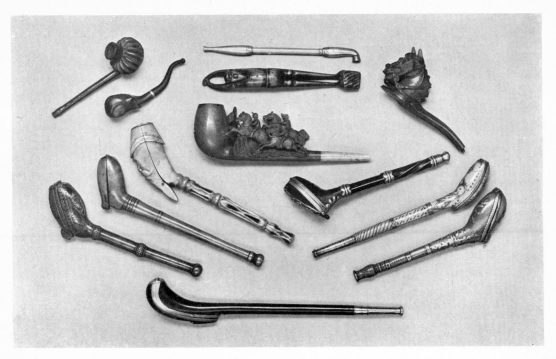

58   Pipe cases, mostly 18th century Dutch, and carved pipes

59   Tobacco jars and boxes.   Below, smokers compendium, cigar cutter, pipe rack, pipe box,
tobacco jar, public-house snuff box and cigarette stand

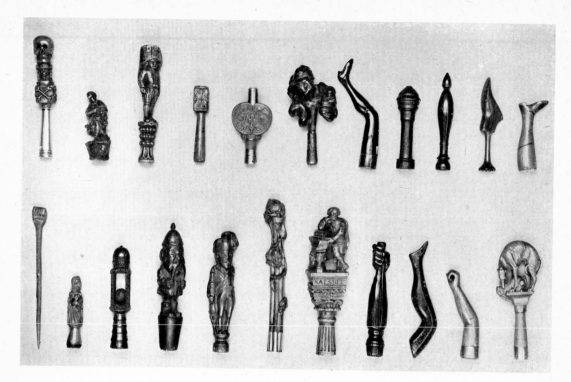

60   A selection of wooden pipe stoppers

61   Cheroot holders and burr cigar and cigarette cases

The French developed a characteristic circular snuff box in the eighteenth and nineteenth centuries, of which eight examples are shown between the rappoirs. All are $3\frac{1}{4}$ to $3\frac{1}{2}$ in. diameter, of birch and, as with mazers, "turned" from root or burr in order to obtain a permanently true circle. All alike have pictures "impressed", not carved, on the face and most have a design in imitation of engine turning impressed on the base. Some have inscriptions in addition. All are beautifully finished and tortoiseshell lined. Some of the best are "sharpened" by carving after pressing. Mostly the scenes or figures depicted are French but a few are English, though of French manufacture. Occasionally these boxes have secret compartments in the base, which may contain Napoleonic or sentimental momentos or lewd pictures. The two boxes (left) are rare "double head" types. Turn the picture round and you will see entirely different faces: the man at the top turns into a horse and the jovial man on the lower box becomes a picture of misery.

In the second column, the top box, with a Watteau shepherdess scene on the lid, contains a secret compartment. The box at the top of the third column, again with secret compartment, has a memento Mori scene on the lid. The lower one is extremely interesting. Entitled "Allegorie sur la bataille des 3 Empereurs", it bears round the border the inscription "Il a vu sans effroi leur violens efforts". It depicts a scene in the centre of which a crowned French eagle, perched on a prostrate German eagle, has seized a double-headed Russian eagle (right) by one claw and is proceeding to pull the feathers from his wings with his beak, having already knocked his crown off; the Prussian lion (left), with tail between legs, is slinking off. Across the sea, in the background, England, in the form of a very complacent bulldog, is shown sitting and watching, with fleet before and the Tower of London behind him.

The two boxes (right) depict the principles of craniology; that at the top shows the various "bumps", which are described on the base of the box. The other box portrays events in the life of Dr. Gall (1758–1828), founder of craniology. The boxes at the bottom are eighteenth century, English; that on the right is of yew wood.

A popular style of snuff box in many parts of Europe during the eighteenth and nineteenth centuries was the shoe, which was generally about 4 in. long and fitted with a hinged or sliding lid on top. Sometimes fancifully carved and inlaid and varying in type from sabot to boot, according to fashion and country of origin (sabot types of boxes are shown in PLATE 130), many of these shoes and boots were made in pairs, as perfect reproductions in miniature of footwear, complete to such details as buttons, metal heels and toe tips and studs. Noteworthy, in the middle row (55) are the third and fourth from left, which are a pair of Victorian button boots of mahogany, inlaid with ebony or stained black between brass piqué lines to represent stitched inserts of patent leather, the soles brass nailed with the date 1884 in a border. The fifth and sixth, of rosewood, are another pair. In the bottom left corner is a $6\frac{1}{2}$ in. long graceful eighteenth-century mahogany shoe, brass piquéd and inlaid with hearts, diamonds and triangles in silver, mother-of-pearl and ebony. The bottom right is a five-button boot with broad, square toe; this box is carved from an attractively figured burry root and is unusual in opening from underneath by pivoting the heel. Top right, the $5\frac{1}{2}$ in. long rosewood shoe has a well-tipped and studded sole and heel. The top left, $6\frac{3}{4}$ in. long, probably early eighteenth century, Flemish, is of walnut, gracefully shaped as a mediæval shoe. It is inlaid with brass piqué, with an ivory relief plaque carved as a bust in sixteenth-century costume. Central at the bottom is a natural birch burr, 6 in. long. The box hollowed out of it opens from the base. The walnut bellows box is probably late seventeenth or early eighteenth century and is brass studded with the initials "M.A.W."

In PLATE 56 are included some unusual snuff boxes. On the shelf (left to right) are a small German "plane" box (obviously some woodworker's charming fancy); a box with an elaborate marquetry of various woods, ivory, green dyed bone and brass, probably Eastern and curious because mounted on a European papier-mâché base; a pensive monkey squatting on its haunches, crudely carved from walnut with snuff receptacle in its back; the bird's-eye maple "book" pattern box, inlaid with a silver heart and a bird and the cylindrical burry root box with ebony lines and tortoiseshell lining are both recognised eighteenth-century types; the walnut box with mother-of-pearl inlay is carved from a solid block; the eighteenth-century oval engine-turned box is of a shape common in silver but unusual in wood, in which it is difficult to execute.

Below (left to right) the seventeenth-century Italian helmet snuff box, of which the peak forms the lid, is made from a burry root with a stained pattern enclosed by piqué lines; the circular box next is an early nineteenth-century French specimen of unusual pattern; the oak circular box has a lead centre plaque, stating that it is made from the roof of York Minster—similar ones also exist made from various other structures, such as the piles of Old London Bridge; the lignum vitæ box lying flat is unusually deep and may have been a tobacco box, the dividing line between small tobacco and large snuff boxes being practically non-existent; the "trick" ring turned box opens by pressing the centre medallion; the round box with geometrical inlay is another which could have been intended for tobacco or snuff; the boxwood "hand" is beautifully made—its "thumb" forms a hinged lid. In front are another cylindrical box and a cushion box with heart inlay. This last is a familiar eighteenth- or early nineteenth-century type.

All the snuff boxes in PLATE 57 are carved from Coquilla nuts, the existence of which seems forgotten in England, as almost invariably they are sold as "burr", "root" or boxwood. Actually they are the nuts of the *attalea funifera* palm, sometimes called the *"Piassaba"* and they have been imported to Europe from South America from the mid-sixteenth century or earlier. They are extremely hard, brittle and polish easily and are characterised by a tortoiseshell-like mottle. Ever since their introduction to Europe, they have been esteemed for turnery and carving, although their absence of long fibres makes them fragile and their oiliness makes repair difficult. Early specimens often formed works of art; later ones were "turned" into the familiar varnished and pierced pomander boxes and pierced "eggs" containing rosaries of the same material, which were sold outside French and Italian churches in Victorian days.

From left to right on the shelf, the first, delicately carved and undercut with mythological subjects is Sicilian, the second Italian, depicting Daniel in the lion's den. Both are early eighteenth-century work. The third is late eighteenth or early nineteenth century, French, and the four grotesques, probably German. The two French boxes (extreme right) have as central motifs on both sides "Romayne heads" and are great rarities, probably made about 1559 when Catherine de Medici received her first parcel of snuff. They are crude and have small irregular cavities, left as formed by removal of the kernels. The foliated bands forming the ends are solid blocks of nut shell dowelled on. Third from the left below is eighteenth century, Dutch; most of the other amusing figures are believed to be late eighteenth and early nineteenth century, German. Advantage is taken of the natural "eyes" in the nuts for pegging the feet on these figures.

TOBACCO PIPES—Whilst briar pipes often have considerable artistic merit, they are disappointing historically as, although so universal to-day, their origin dates back little more than a century. From the mid-sixteenth century until 1821, the clay was universal, only challenged by porcelain and meerschaum in the wealthiest households. The costliness of tobacco, when first introduced, resulted in pipe bowls being minute and generally clays can be dated approximately by size, which increased as tobacco cheapened.

Further aids to dating are that early pipes had flat "heels" so that they rested upright on a table. "Spurs" came in about 1780–90 and "Aldermen", with longer stems tipped with glaze, were a fashion of Queen Anne's reign. "Churchwardens" were an early nineteenth-century introduction.

According to Alfred Dunhill, the discovery that briar, which incidentally has nothing to do with rose briar, was the ideal material for pipes, occurred fortuitously. In the mid-nineteenth century, a French pipe maker on a pilgrimage to the birthplace of Napoleon in Corsica, lost or broke his meerschaum pipe there. A peasant, at his request, carved him a new one of wood for temporary use, utilising the hard, fine-grained root of the tree-heath or bruyère, which grows around both shores of the Mediterranean. The pipe was so successful that the manufacturer took home some bruyère roots and thus revolutionised pipe manufacture. In PLATE 58 are some interesting specimens. The pipe with the three jockeys riding at a fence is an example of elaboration of ornament marring usefulness, but it is a fine carving. The same remarks apply, in lesser degree, to the horse. The elephant pipe is modern from Ceylon and the one-piece example with radiating fins is Zulu, designed most practically for comfortable handling in a tropical climate. The long-legged gentleman forms a rack for the cane-stemmed, silver-mounted opium pipe alongside. When not in use, it nests under him with the mouthpiece through his arms and the bowl clipped in the block under his feet.

PIPE CASES—Most pipes being clay until the nineteenth century necessitated protection against breakage in the pocket. English cases were generally plain and of birch, sometimes inlaid in dots or incised with the owner's initials; the best, like the Dutch and German, were often of boxwood, ebony or walnut. Seven specimens, mostly eighteenth century, Dutch or German, are in PLATE 58. That on the left, of boxwood, dated 1756, is finely carved with a coat of arms, a boy skipping, a grotesque head and a heart containing the initials "K.M." The top left of boxwood, with pierced stem to show the clay through, is an early nineteenth-century specimen. The top right of ebony has a secret spring for opening the lid. It and the three below are all brass-mounted.

PIPE RACKS AND BOXES—Much ingenuity has been exercised in these smoker's appurtenances. In the eighteenth century, churchwarden boxes were common; the one illustrated (59) is unusual in having at the end an enclosed compartment for tinder and steel. Also used were combined candlesticks and vertical pipe racks, which were particularly sensible for evenings, when the candle combined illumination and pipe lighting. Other forms of holders were wall racks, for holding churchwarden pipes horizontally. The quaint nineteenth-century pipe rack in front of the pipe box includes in its design carved heads of a bulldog, a rhinoceros, a monkey, a fox and a wolf.

TOBACCO JARS—The majority of old tobacco jars were lead, some pewter, brass and pottery and a small number treen, usually with lead or lead foil liners. Old treen jars or boxes are rare, very varied in design and often confused with small tea caddies. The small caddies, however, were only used when tea was an expensive luxury; consequently, nearly all have locks, whilst tobacco jars do not. Unfortunately this test is not infallible, because some tea caddies had no locks, consequent on their being fitted into a lock-up case or tea-poy (fitted table).

Left to right on the shelf (59) are two Georgian mahogany jars, the first of which recalls designs of eighteenth-century standing cups and the second that of mortars; the third, a modern piece $8\frac{1}{2}$ in. high, is spiritedly carved and lightly stained in natural colours and is a variant of those eighteenth-century jars which were formed as negro heads for holding tobacco of the same name. The fourth is a nineteenth-century

Scottish table box, crudely carved from a solid sycamore block, including the hinges. The lid shows a man on horseback wearing a tam-o'-shanter and talking to a shepherd dressed in plaid. On the front edge are two sheep guarded by a sheep dog on each end. The fifth, the rather sharp oval box, is also carved from a solid block and is a ship's tobacco box. Below, the attractive eighteenth-century miniature wassail bowl of yew wood, $7\frac{3}{8}$ in. high, was probably made for a tobacco jar.

PIPE STOPS—These charming little trifles for pressing down tobacco in the pipe seem to have disappeared from fashion during the past century. Some writers before the 1914–18 war suggested that cheap tobacco had eliminated the need for stoppers to husband the last dregs of tobacco. This may be partially so, as tobacco then only cost $4\frac{1}{2}d.$ to $5d.$ per oz.; that reason certainly does not apply to-day! Moreover, the end of the pipeful is not the only time when a stopper may be required to adjust the "draw" by pressing down the tobacco.

Seventeenth- to nineteenth-century literature proves that pewter, silver, bronze and carved wood and bone pipe stoppers were commonly used and the last two provided scope for the skill and imagination of anyone handy with knife and chisel. Many metal but few treen specimens have survived, however, and the latter are now so rare that well-carved specimens, originally costing pennies, now fetch pounds. This applies particularly to those which were made to commemorate events or notabilities, such as the Duke of Wellington, a fanatical non-smoker, who made himself a notorious "pipe stopper" by an edict forbidding soldiers smoking in barracks.

In PLATE 60 is an unusually large and varied selection of wooden specimens and it will be seen how popular were arm and leg motifs. Generally stoppers with small "stamps", like the first six (left to right of upper row), were early ones to suit the small bowled pipes.

The following are particularly noteworthy. Left to right, top row, the first, of silver-mounted boxwood, shows a skull above an hour glass, inscribed "Memento Mori"; the cube below is carved on its four sides with a coffin, cross bones, crossed spade and mattock and initials "I.I.G." and date 1715. The second, the boxwood statuette of a Stuart flower girl, shows signs of burning and use, but it is doubtful if it were designed as a stopper. The third is a highly skilled boxwood carving, dated 1720 and interesting as a costume piece of the reign of George I. The fifth, the silver-mounted bellows, is an eighteenth-century unusual form. Next is a root formation, pewter-mounted.

In the bottom row, from the left, the first is a thornwood tobacco pricker. The second is coquilla nut, delicately carved with a woman's head surmounting figures of an angel, a man with a musket and a woman with a book. The third, with ball and lantern, is eighteenth century, English or Welsh. The fourth, Bismarck, though much burnt, probably commenced life as a bottle stopper. The fifth, the soldier, portrays uniform of about 1785. The sixth is probably unique, being carved from a vine stem, the natural features of which have been shaped into grotesque beasts and heads. Next, the finely composed "Shakespeare" stopper is boxwood and depicts the Master leaning on the volumes of his works, placed on a pedestal supported by busts of Henry V, Richard II and Queen Elizabeth. Several versions of this subject are extant, all carved by Salsbee, who proudly announces on the plinth of this one that he cut it in 1774 when aged 71. Correspondence on these Salsbee Shakespeare figures occurred in various issues of *The Antique Collector* in 1943. Two statuettes of Shakespeare, not pipe stops, were illustrated and I know of three Shakespeare pipe stops including my own, so evidently this particular figure was the *chef d'œvre* of old Salsbee. All these statuettes are based on the standing figure of Shakespeare in Westminster Abbey by Peter

Scheemakers (1691–1770). Despite being copies, each reproduction has some quaint variation and individuality imparted by the carver. Unfortunately the correspondence has not produced any personal details of Salsbee. Extreme right is a silver-mounted boxwood greyhound coursing a hare, a popular eighteenth-century subject. Others which are found occasionally include hearts, anvils, bottles and glasses, monkeys with coconuts and squirrels with nuts. The Shakespeare, ball and lantern, silver-mounted arm and leg and root stoppers were formerly in the Owen Evan-Thomas collection.

Whilst there must have been a regular industry in pipe stoppers, a number of the most fascinating were undoubtedly carved by gifted amateurs and frequent references to this hobby occur in contemporary fiction. Dickens, in *Great Expectations*, makes mention of several tobacco stoppers carved by Wemmick's deaf and "Aged Parent". Addison also, in the original *Spectator*, refers to Sir Roger de Coverley's friend, Will Wimble, and his habit of turning out great quantities of tobacco stoppers during the winter months, for presentation to his friends "who had good principles and smoked"!

CHEROOT CASKETS, CIGAR CUTTERS AND MISCELLANEOUS—As previously mentioned, the reduction in the tobacco tax at the commencement of the nineteenth century and the taste for cigars introduced by the military who had acquired the habit in Spain during the Peninsular war of 1807–14, caused a switch from snuffing to smoking. This resulted in many ingenious designs for caskets, some of which displayed their contents semi-mechanically, by operating a knob or lever.

Two interesting specimens, both approximately 9 in. high, are shown open (61). Each is actuated by turning the knob on top, but the English example (left) revolves by means of cord driven beechwood wheels in the base, while the French model (right) has wooden cogs. The former holds six cheroots and is mahogany, "japanned" with flowers on a black background, to harmonise with the papier-mâché in vogue about 1850. The French cabinet, dating from about 1820, is veneered with kingwood and ebony, ormolu-mounted and has holders for fifteen cheroots, arranged in groups of three, the side facing the camera being reserved for a combined cigar piercer, matchbox and striker.

The Karelian birch burr one-piece cigar case and cigarette case of the same wood, on which it stands, are fine quality examples of twentieth-century treen. The polychrome painted cigar cutter, portraying Mephistopheles, next to the barrel on stand (59), is still giving good service. The barrel provides an unusual combination: the barrel, lead lined, may have held tobacco, snuff or "whiffs" and its tap is a cigar cutter, the guillotined ends falling into the bucket, which originally probably had a loose liner. A match striker is on the front of the base. The wood is pear, finished mahogany colour and brass-mounted. The date is about 1870.

✱   ✱   ✱

COLLECTORS NOTES

Many museums contain specimens of treen connected with tobacco, but I know of no comprehensive collection.

Magnificent examples of snuff boxes are in the British Museum, the Wallace Collection and the Victoria and Albert Museum, but the majority are not treen. The latter possesses a fine collection of silver, ivory and treen rappoirs and outstanding examples of carved boxwood pipe cases. The Wallace Collection has a particularly fine Louis XIV rappoir, about 13 ins. long, carved with figures of Theophane and the ram, and Diana.

Messrs. W. D. & H. O. Wills have at their Bedminster, Bristol, factory a unique collection of pipes in many materials, including not only many finely carved wood specimens, but also such weird contraptions as an Austrian single bowl cherry pipe, pierced by three stems diverging, so that it could be smoked by three people at the same time.

Museum No. 3 of the Royal Botanic Gardens, Kew, contains a good collection of pipes from many lands, made from many woods.

PART SEVEN

ACCESSORIES FOR READING AND WRITING

READING

ENGLISH learning commenced in the monasteries. The monks not only read books, they made them, and until the introduction of printing, the majority of beautifully illuminated manuscripts and sumptuously bound books were their work. By the twelfth century, if not earlier, all great monasteries had their scriptoria for writing and painting, and cloisters for reading. Against one cloister wall stood "almeries" or cupboards for books, whilst opposite, each monk had his separate "carrell" or pew, fitted with seat and sloping reading desk. Fifteenth-century monasteries and colleges had libraries fitted in the modern manner with desks like church lecterns, to which volumes in use were chained; bibles in churches were similarly secured.

The more general distribution of learning following the introduction of printing in the fifteenth century and the dissolution of the monasteries in the sixteenth made libraries less a special church appurtenance, but not until the seventeenth century had reading become general enough to create demand for special-purpose furniture. The eighteenth century saw the heyday of ingenious library steps which converted into chairs or cabinets, of library tables with special reading attachments, reading tables with rise, fall and tilting actions, adjustable book rests and swing reading brackets.

TRAVELLING LIBRARIES—A lesser known example of eighteenth-century cabinet-maker's craft was the travelling library, used by the student going to college, or travellers on land or sea. A good example in mahogany, with wired doors in the "Gothic" taste, is in PLATE 62. Closed, it forms an 18-in. cube. The corners and angles are protected with brass. The back and front, each framed up to form four sunk panels, have heavy brass carrying handles.

BOOK RESTS—Many were provided with candle brackets and, being luxuries, are invariably quality pieces. An ingeniously made eighteenth-century mahogany folding book rest of good proportions, with ratchet angle adjustment, appears open in PLATE 63 and closed right of PLATE 62. It measures $8\frac{3}{4}$ by $6\frac{3}{4}$ by $\frac{9}{16}$ in. when closed.

THE HORN BOOK—Bookbinding, wood cut and wood engraved blocks for printing are discussed in Part 14 but, appropriate to this section, there is a book which is often mainly treen. It is the "Horn Book", about which an exhaustive and beautifully bound historical book was written by a Mr. Tuer in 1896. In early days, printing was so costly and books so rare that none seems to have been designed especially for nursery teaching before the reign of Charles II.

The earliest recorded child educator was the above-mentioned horn book, horn bat, or battledore book, which was introduced about 1450 and continued in use until about 1800. Mr. Tuer's research unearthed 150 horn books, most of which went to America, and genuine specimens are now so rare that a collector is unlikely to find one, but in no other branch of treen is he more liable to acquire a fake. Central bottom of PLATE 98 appears a typical fake—a warning of what not to buy. It bears carved initials and the date MR. 3 1592 on the back, and considerable misguided effort has been expended on "ageing". Horn Books generally are shaped like battledores or dressing table hand mirrors. Wooden examples usually have their lettering covered by a horn sheet, secured

62 A writing board and a Welsh peithynen above a Georgian travelling library. *In front*, ink wells, pencil box, seals and a doll string box

63 A Georgian folding book rest, string boxes and thorn pins

64 Ink wells, signets, seal boxes, ink horn and quill cutter

65　Pounce boxes, paper weights and miscellanea of the writing table

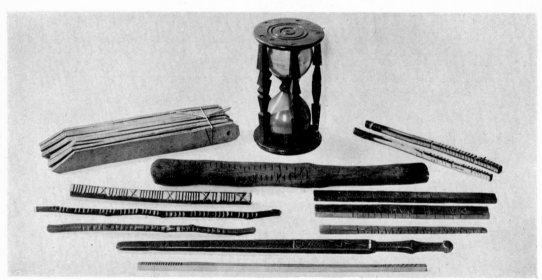

66　An hour glass and tally sticks

67　Measures of capacity

68   Various weighing and measuring devices.   The 17th century diamond merchant scales (*extreme right*) are superb quality.   So also is the inlaid ell rule dated 1656

69   Boxwood microscope, a stethoscope, scales, and an apothecary's mortar and chopping board

70   Six varieties of mortars and an early slide rule

71   A nest of seventeen Mexican carved measures, 18th century

by a narrow brass frame. The fake illustrated is poor and is covered with mica secured by a nail-studded parchment strip. It displays the alphabet and numerals inscribed on parchment, as often occurs on genuine specimens. Sometimes the signs are engraved direct into the wood and followed by the Lord's Prayer, or a verse reading:

"Christe's Cross be my speede
In all virtue to proceede"

To the public, the term "horn book" eventually signified an alphabet tablet, and the term horn book was often given erroneously to its successor, the "A B C" book or primer. As mentioned in Part 3, when horn books were used generally, they were so much part of children's lives that gingerbread counterparts were sold at fairs.

An Arabic wooden "slate" or writing tablet is shown left above the travelling library (62).

THE PEITHYNEN—The Welsh invented the real "book of treen", known as a peithynen or LLYFR PREN—Wooden Book, illustrated on the right (62) above the bookcase. It consists of a frame containing a number of revolving three-, four- or six-sided sticks, carved with numerals, the alphabet, the Lord's Prayer, or bardic verses. Characters, normally curved, appear angular on a peithynen, for easy notching out with a knife. The peithynen's claim to great antiquity is not borne out by investigation and it seems to have been largely a hoax, perpetrated by Iolo Morgannwg and his associates in the eighteenth century. Sir John Morris Jones exposes its fraudulence in *A Welsh Grammar* (1913), pointing out that it could never have served a serious purpose since a cartload of wooden books would be required to cover the contents of a small manuscript volume.

WRITING

Specialised writing treen is rarely found antedating the eighteenth century and most of that extant is nineteenth century; inkstands particularly are scarce. This is not due to any shortage of letter writers—in fact, the contrary; probably never were they more prolific or verbose. The reason is that the country was divided into a large majority suffering grinding poverty and illiteracy and a small leisured class, wealthier and better educated than ever before, who preferred silver or at least pewter to wood for their writing accessories. Admittedly, between the extremes was a layer of country squires, professional folk and successful tradesmen, and it is these we must thank for most eighteenth-century writing treen. When one reads the voluminous correspondence of the times, notes the elegant and flowery literary compositions and fine handwriting and considers the tools with which our ancestors laboured, it is apparent that considerable leisure and patience were necessary adjuncts. There were no typewriters, fountain pens, steel pens, blotting paper, gummed envelopes or artificial light except candles (I speak feelingly on the difficulties of writing by candlelight; the early stages of this book are being written by that fitful illumination, due to the unusual severity of this winter and shortage of fuel and power—February, 1947).

PENS—Before it was used to describe a goose quill specifically prepared for writing, the word "pen" simply meant a feather. Quill pens were formerly peddled from door to door. A sixteenth-century series of woodcuts of "Cries" in the British Museum contains the "Pen and Ink Man" (No. 11) with ink bottle slung on his pedlar's stick and a bunch of quills in his hand, while he cries:

> *"Buy pens, pens, pens of the best,*
> *Excellent pens and seconds the least;*
> *Come buy good ink as black as jet,*
> *A varnish like gloss on writing 'twill set."*

The penknife, in those days, was a tool of great importance and, consequently, its case was sometimes a real work of art. A sixteenth-century gem, probably unique, is the Italian folding penknife in PLATE 45.

Early in the nineteenth century, the ingenious device lying on its original case, in front of the card box (left, 64), was invented. It is of ebony and the end nearest the camera forms a socket for an extending knife blade, which roughly shaped the quill. The hinged brass lever at the opposite end contains a sharp edged steel cutter which, when pressed on a quill inserted in it, not only cuts the correct profile of a nib, but also divides it by means of a central razor-edged blade. The ebony handle contains a third compartment in which the nib is then inserted for cutting the point off to give the thickness of writing desired by the scribe. A small brass slot in the handle, like that in the head of a screw, was used for bending the end of the nib upwards. Wise of London made the first steel pens in 1803.

PEN AND INK STANDS—The predecessors of inkpots were ink wells of leather and inkhorns which were used throughout the Middle Ages and until the late sixteenth century. An inkhorn is on the extreme right of PLATE 64.

In the seventeenth and eighteenth centuries, inkstands or "standishes" of pewter or silver were in domestic use. Usually they consisted of a plateau which held one or more inkpots, a pounce box and one or two pen wells or pots. Some had, moreover, a pen wiper, a bell, a seal holder and one or two candlesticks. Some eighteenth-century stands were of mahogany, with a drawer in the plateau, above which were arranged glass or silver ink bottles and pounce box and one or two pen wells or racks. Stands which have their ink and pounce pots in a centre line, with pen wells or racks on each side, were intended for the centre of a partner's desk. Wooden inkstands made between 1840 and 1900 are not difficult to find as yet and some are made from rare woods, beautifully mounted and polished and are altogether unusually good examples of nineteenth-century design and workmanship. These two-bottle inkstands cannot be confused with earlier specimens because, due to the invention of blotting paper at approximately the earlier date, the pounce box is omitted. Usually they have two glass inkpots, a central domed casket for seals, etc., one or two pen wells and sometimes a deep storage well under the centre plateau or a secret drawer.

Offices and more humble homes used inkwells of pewter or wood. A late eighteenth-century ring-turned ebony inkwell is near the left of PLATE 64. Next is a Regency walnut penwiper bucket, decorated with brass ornamentation and right are two nineteenth-century lignum vitæ ink wells, carved to simulate basketware. The larger has circular apertures in the rim, to hold pens. In PLATE 62 are three more ink wells; one in the form of a much worn boot has the hinged lid carved to represent a tucked-in sock. To right of the boot is a domed souvenir ink well case, of laminated wood, made about 1820–40 and left a modern Australian specimen in Crown Mulgawood.

POUNCE BOXES—Blotting paper was discovered accidentally at Hagbourne Mill, Berkshire, where John Slade made paper by hand. About the year 1840, some workmen omitted the essential ingredients of "size" from the manufacture, resulting in a quantity of apparent waste. Luckily someone wrote a note on a piece of the "waste" and the outcome was "Slade's Original Hand Made Blotting", which soon received the seal of approval by being used regularly by Queen Victoria. The Slade business passed by marriage to Thomas Ford, and now all the world knows "Ford's Blotting".

Gummed envelopes seem to have been introduced almost simultaneously with blotting paper and as 1840 also saw the country-wide extension of the penny postage (established in London in 1683), it was a momentous time for letter writers.

Before that date, having sharpened our quill and having written our letter, we sanded it with pounce, sprinkled from one of the pounce boxes (left, 65). We then "cupped" our writing paper and poured the pounce back into the saucer-shaped rim of the pounce box, whence, by means of the sprinkler holes, it returned to the container. The four pounce boxes illustrated are all eighteenth-century English specimens. That on the left, of fruitwood, is the earliest. The others are of lignum vitæ. Pounce was made from powdered cuttle fish or pumice powder.

SEALS—Before gummed envelopes were invented, the missive was folded, addressed and, after sanding, sealed by means of candle, sealing wax and impress of one of the seals or signets (64).

Some of these signets, notably the lignum vitæ example standing on the left and the one with its lid lying alongside, have receptacles in the handles for gummed "wafers", which were used in conjunction with them. The seal lying front left claims that it was Lord Brougham's, made from the oak beams of York Minster. The detail of the ebony signet standing left of the centre does not show clearly; it is beautifully carved with a lioness in a tree, preparing to pounce on a bird. The disgruntled looking man next to it is finely carved from boxwood, dated 1819 and unusual in having the seal engraved on unprotected wood. The boxwood ball and lantern signet, extreme right, with a shoe forming the handle, is a rare specimen, probably seventeenth century. Two more signets are in PLATE 62; one takes the form of a well-carved bulldog head; the other, of coquilla nut and ivory, contains a receptacle for "wafers".

Specimen wax seals were always kept in specially made ebony or lignum vitæ turned boxes, a number of which are in front of PLATE 64.

STRING BOXES—If our letter were being despatched in a parcel, we had to wrap and string it before sealing. The eighteenth and nineteenth centuries provided a considerable variety of treen string boxes. A number are in PLATE 63. The barrel types were invariably well-finished and have a knob on the top or end, which actuates the wooden spool inside. The string emerges through the "tap" and is cut by a knife blade fixed on it. The centre barrel shown is boxwood, the other two lignum vitæ. The lignum vitæ "brick" pattern engine-turned box and the ring-turned boxwood beehive, with cutter on top, are late eighteenth or early nineteenth century. The lignum vitæ beehive, next to the book rest, is a commoner nineteenth-century pattern, which was also made in large sizes for shop use. The commonest late nineteenth-century shop pattern is the large lignum vitæ box on the right.

On the extreme left, the ebonised box, with brass and celluloid ornaments, is a hideous pattern popular about 1870. An amusing and rather charming specimen, reminiscent in its design of slipware of about 1740, is the lady in PLATE 62; her dress is painted in an ivory shade with spots and cuffs of primrose yellow.

PAPER WEIGHTS—Paper weights are diverse enough to form a specific collection. In PLATE 65 are four treen specimens. The nineteenth-century oval one, with knob handle, from the North-West Province of India, is finely inlaid with tárkashi brass work. Right, Thorwaldsen's lion of Lucerne, carved from walnut and lead weighted, is too familiar to need description. To prevent more copies appearing in my study, may I say that it has haunted me for years: as soon as I give one away, someone sends me another!

The miniature Sheraton serpentine fronted cutlery box in front is perfect in detail; it is carved from a block of mahogany and is lead weighted. So also is that representing a concertina envelope, with strap and buckle carved from the solid. Another example of this technique is the stationery box (left, 64).

PENCILS—Pencil, like pen, is a word which has changed its meaning. The original pencil was the brush used for lettering manuscripts. When the newcomer, our pencil, arrived, probably in the sixteenth century, it was called a blacklead, to distinguish it. The propelling pencil was introduced by Hawkins and Mordan in 1822. An early wooden specimen, with bone ends, shown in PLATE 65, is stamped "Lund Patent London" and has "V.R." and the crown engraved on it; the lead is actuated by a silver collar, the spirals of which travel in the matching spirals in the exterior of the wood cylinder.

PENCIL BOXES—Edwardian pencil boxes, in use when I first went to school, seem to have disappeared; soon they will be collectors' pieces. Most intriguing they were too, carved from a single block, circular at the ends. They were in three tiers, pivoted at one end, with numerous quaint little compartments, the whole box of tricks locking together by a sliding lid. A Victorian penny pencil box appears in PLATE 62, a nineteenth-century cylindrical pencil box from North-West Europe in PLATE 130 and one made from bamboo, cut with interlocking prongs and engraved with an early nineteenth-century view of a busy Eastern port, is in PLATE 65.

MISCELLANEOUS—The Victorian walnut sheath, in the same picture, must have given pleasure to some child, with its pen, pencil, penknife and paper knife all terminating in fox-terrier head carvings. A paper knife, with the handle carved with delicately undercut and natural coloured sprays of flowers and leaves, appears in the foreground.

The two remaining objects in PLATE 65 are a wood mosaic Italian ruler and the cylindrical wooden vessel near the right, which is a travelling combination. It has a seal on top, the uppermost compartment holds an inkpot, the middle one sealing wafers and the base a pounce box.

A collection of *Babla* pins, made from natural thorns and still in normal use in India for pinning papers, are on a tray in front of PLATE 63.

*   *   *

COLLECTORS NOTES

The Royal Albert Memorial Museum, Exeter, preserves the wooden seal of Blewbury, whilst Dorset County Museum, Dorchester, has three rare exhibits—cylindrical turned wooden boxes with lids fastened by raw hide thongs. They are probably fifteenth century and were used for holding small deeds in the library at Wimbourne Minster.

Apart from numerous examples of pounce boxes in various museums and Tunbridgeware inkstands, pen trays, paper knives, etc., in the museums at Tunbridge Wells and Brighton, I cannot recollect any outstanding examples of reading and writing treen in public collections.

PART EIGHT

RECKONING, MEASURING, GRINDING
AND MIXING

TALLIES—At first glance the connection between wood "tallies" and parliament is not apparent, but the "teller" was originally the "tallier" and tallies were so important in parliamentary recording that burning some of their accumulation caused the fire which destroyed the Houses of Parliament in 1834.

For many centuries (actually until 1783) tallies were used in the English Court of Exchequer as receipts for money paid to officials and in less literate ages they were used universally in most European countries for recording cash owed, votes cast, hay cut, corn reaped, fish caught, goods carried, sheep sheared, etc. Their use now is practically extinct, though they serve in a small way for hop-picking records.

Tallies, though not decorative, possess much interest, as PLATE 66 shows. The method of use was simple. Notches to represent figures were cut transversely on the stick, which was made from any suitable local wood. The notches varied either in breadth, length, spacing or angle of cut to denote differences between pounds, shillings and pence, or between lbs., cwts. and tons, etc. When the particular transaction was completed, the stick was split centrally through all the notches, one half being retained by each party until settlement was effected. Where records involved payments, specially prepared tally sticks were used to avoid any argument as to which party was the lender. Before the nineteenth century, each stick was prepared specifically for a transaction, but from about 1800 commercial manufacture appears to have been instituted. A bundle of ready prepared commercial hop tallies is at back left of PLATE 66. They are sawn through for about five-sixths of their length the long cut nearly but not quite meeting the horizontal cut. After use, with the required notches representing the transaction cut transversely at intervals right across the long saw cut and the names of the contracting parties recorded on the stick, the two "halves" were broken apart. The lender retained the long "half", called the "stock" or "tally" and the short "half", named the "counter-stock" or "counter-tally", belonged to the borrower.

For some time after wooden tallies were superseded, cheques, tickets and other documents were torn by an irregular line of separation, the "tallying" of the torn edges being accepted as validity of claim.

The two tallies (right, 66) are Herefordshire farm labourers' tallies. The notches right across represent a full day's work; the short nicks equal half-days. The central $16\frac{1}{2}$ in. long heavy round section tally is from Kirkcudbright, Scotland. The two "wavy" sticks (left), 14 and $11\frac{1}{2}$ in. long respectively, were for numbering prayers at pilgrim stations on Holy Island, Barra. The 15-in. tally (front) from Llanwrtyd, Brecknock, records sheep, divided as 210 lambs, 78 wethers and 18 rams.

SAND GLASSES—The references above to measuring prayers leads to the lesser known sand glasses. The usual one-hour type (66), with turned wood baluster connected ends, is only a larger form of egg timer, but there were intermediate sizes, usually quarter or half-hour glasses which, mounted on pivoted brackets in sets of two or four above the pulpit, were used in country churches to measure "parson's sermon". The most interesting I have seen are 13 half-hour glasses in the collection of Mr. and Mrs. T. W. Bagshawe. Originally numbering 18, these were bought from a York dealer, who unfortunately had sold five separately. They were used daily by the nuns at St. Mary's Convent, York, until about A.D. 1900, when use of watches was first permitted there.

WEIGHTS AND MEASURES—Measurements, whether linear, gravimetric or volumetric, must always be based on ascertaining how often a standard quantity is contained in some unknown quantity. In this class of treen, therefore, accuracy and serviceability of the standard have generally been placed before art. Nevertheless, as the illustrations show, our ancestors sometimes combined fine art without detracting from utility.

In early days, common objects served as measures, as is evident from the dual meaning of such words as hand (4 in.), foot (12 in.), pennyweight, etc. In 1101, in an effort at standardisation, Henry I is said to have decreed that the length of his arm should define the yard. Presumably the nautical term "yard-arm" survived from this. It appears that Henry defined his arm as extending from finger-tip to middle of chest, because the fathom, 72 in., was originally the distance between the extremities of extended arms. A check on these standards shows that Henry had the average reach of a modern man.

The pennyweight was founded on the penny, which was defined in 1266 as an "English peny called a sterling, round and without clipping, which shall weigh thirty-two wheat corns from the midst of the ear". The word sterling is a contraction of Easterling. "Easterlings" were a Guild of North German traders who settled in London in the reign of Edward I and produced their own coinage. Their coins, of uniformly high quality, under the title of "sterling", became recognised as a reliable standard.

LINEAR MEASURES—Before the wide adoption of the metric system on the continent, the ell was a popular measure, particularly for cloth, both here and abroad. Its wide variation in length in different countries must have proved troublesome as in England it was officially 45 in., in Scotland 37·2 in., while the Flemish ell measured only 27 in.

The magnificent Western German short ell rule (front, 68), formerly in the Trapnall collection, is now owned by Mr. H. Baer. Of triangular section, boxwood, inlaid with ivory and mother-of-pearl on all faces, it measures $21\frac{1}{4}$ in. Engraved in ivory at one end is the date 1656. The reverse end bears the initials "G.H." above the figure of a mounted knight. The length is divided as follows. From left to right, the first two sections on each side measure $1\frac{1}{4}$ in.; then follow three sections each of $2\frac{3}{4}$ in. and finally two sections each $5\frac{1}{4}$ in. long. The six $1\frac{1}{4}$ in. panels are all inlaid with floral motifs. The nine $2\frac{3}{4}$ in. panels have scenes which show kings, queens and knaves, as well as monkeys, lions, rabbits, goats and greyhounds. The first three $5\frac{1}{4}$ in. panels show respectively a goat and a bull charging on a shield in which is depicted a man shooting with a bow and arrow, two grotesque animals playing cards and two other grotesque animals holding a shield engraved with a pair of scissors. The last three panels contain formal arrangements of fruit and flowers.

Immediately behind is a crude rule inscribed "Ana Getz 1804". Apparently it was for teaching a child, as one side of the triangular section is engraved with the alphabet.

A pocket "size stick", used for measuring the foot in shoe fitting, is in PLATE 114 and a waist measurer in PLATE 118.

CALCULATING DEVICES—One of the earliest and most widely adopted calculating devices still used is that termed in England a "ball frame" and in the United States an "adder". It is the familiar rectangular wooden frame of the nursery, holding parallel wires on which movable coloured wooden balls are used to teach children to count. Early civilisations knew it as the "Abacus" and it was used for general calculations by the ancient Greeks, Romans, Egyptians, Hindus and Mexicans and is still used in Japan, in China where it is called the "Suan-Pan" and in Russia, where it is called the "Stchoty". In most of these countries the abacus for adult use has flattened spherical balls of plain, uncoloured wood, mounted on wooden rods.

The invention of logarithms by John Napier (1550–1617) paved the way for that much more scientific calculating device, the slide rule. There were various intermediate stages and Napier provided the first in the year of his death—a small case containing a series of boxwood rods with numerical tables on them, known as "Napier's bones". These were improved by Gaspard Schott, who in 1668 converted the four-sided rods into revolving cylinders.

The first calculating rule based on scientific principles and direct ancestor of modern slide rules, was produced by Gunter in 1620. It was a single scale which needed compasses for calculating. The present two part rule was invented six years later by Wingate. More than two and a quarter centuries elapsed before Mannheim, a Frenchman, in 1850–1 added the now universal cursor. This time lag is curious because cursors were known early in the seventeenth century and their advantage on slide rules was recognised by Newton. An unusually early specimen, 18 in. long, is one from the front of PLATE 70. It has four sections—the main body and three slides. As well as being a normal slide rule for multiplication, division, squares, cubes, etc., it contains numerous other scales relating specifically to vintners' and brewers' calculations. Among many headings engraved on it are:

> 2d. variety; Malt Wash to LW; Cyder to Couch; Divisers for Ale, Wine, etc.; Gauge Points for Ale, Wine, Malt and various other vintner's constants.

Because the rule is engraved with the name "Owen Gill", its owner, and "Edward Roberts of Dove Court, Old Jewry", its maker, it has proved possible to trace its history through the courtesy of the Worshipful Company of Vintners. About the year 1775 a Mr. William Gill evolved a system of ascertaining varying contents of casks and various vintner's constants by using slides and he commissioned Edward Roberts to make them. As far as can be traced, only six were made, as they were quickly proved inaccurate. The six were eventually used by some enterprising wine merchants, obviously including Owen Gill, who was presumably related to the inventor; these merchants are supposed to have toyed with rule and cask in order to impress their importance upon their customers.

MEASURES OF CAPACITY—A mural painting in the tomb of Hesy, an overseer in Egypt 3000 B.C., shows a set of wooden measures for grain, and copper measures for liquids, which might have been made to-day. The painted detail is so perfect that it clearly depicts fourteen graduating wooden measures as having pine staves and black bands. Even the wooden "strike" for levelling off heaped grain from the top of the measure is identical to ones used to-day.

All old English measures which I have seen are stamped and verified by an inspector of weights and measures, with a crown and initials of the reigning sovereign. Precisely when this form of stamping originated is unknown, but a statute of William the Conqueror ordained that measures and weights should be true and stamped, in all parts of the Kingdom.

The three largest (67), a $\frac{1}{4}$, $\frac{1}{2}$ and 1 peck, the three in front of them on the left and the two extreme right of the back row are all Victorian. The brass-rimmed example (back row) is a George III specimen. The double egg-cup type measures, in the medium sizes sometimes erroneously described as hen- and duck-egg cups, are boxwood, of a pattern which occurs commonly in eighteenth-century pewter. All these were usually made in sets. The iron-bound set is of steamed oak, all the handled measures beech and the goblet pattern mahogany. Owing to their gradual shrinkage, solid turned wood measures were not accepted for verification in England after 1907.

In measures of capacity, as in measures of length, artistic finish occurs occasionally; a fine example is the set of eighteenth-century Mexican measures (71). The seventeen vessels nest into each other, the largest and smallest being each closed with a cover. All exterior surfaces are carved with floral scrollwork, partly interlacing, amid which are crowned lions and other animals, birds and insects. The set is $11\frac{1}{4}$ in. high overall and diameter $9\frac{1}{4}$ in. Somewhat similar sets are found in bronze, but I have seen no other fine treen specimens.

WEIGHING APPLIANCES—The origin of measuring by weighing and its connection with Justice are lost in antiquity. In the Bible are at least eleven references to weighing in the balance. The Greeks, Romans, Egyptians and Chinese before the Christian Era too, used metal scales in wooden boxes. Complete fitted boxes of almost exactly similar pattern to that used 200 years ago have been found in Egypt by Professor Flinders Petrie; they are of Roman workmanship and 1,600 years old. Probably the ancients also used all-wood scales. In England, until the nineteenth century, they were common for weighing butter in the dairy. An example is in PLATE 52. Metal hand balances, with turned dishes of beech, similar to the eighteenth-century example suspended in PLATE 68, were used for weighing many commodities.

A type of steelyard in which the point of balance is moved, is called a "bismar". Sometimes made of wood and used in England until the fifteenth century for weighing wool and silk, it so lent itself to cheating that in 1450 the Archbishop of Canterbury decreed excommunication of anyone possessing it. The device continued in use in the Orkney and Shetland Islands until a century ago and is still used in China and Japan.

Specialised and ingeniously constructed scales for money and precious stones were made from mediæval times. The finest specimen I have seen is the pair of diamond merchant's scales in walnut case (right, 68). It is Italian, in the fine art class and dates from about 1650. The beam, needle and fulcrum are steel, the standard and base brass and scale pans silver. As shown, the scales are constructed for erecting in their case, the height of the pans being adjusted by moving forward the brass lion in the foreground, which pulls on a silk cord passing over four brass pulley wheels set in the standard. The walnut case, which has a hand-coloured engraved pastoral scene in the lid, is carved in well-contrived simulation of tooled leather, fashionable at that time, when some boxes were shaped and carved to imitate two volumes. It measures 10 by 6 in. The fine workmanship of the exterior is shown in PLATE 113. The concave slide in the front edge is designed to hold forceps.

Central in PLATE 68 is a pair of money hand-balances in mahogany case. The scale pans bear the maker's initials "D.C." and inside the lid is a label stating "All sorts of beams and scales sold by Dan¹, Crosby at the sign of the Crown and Scales, Pill Lane, Dublin". The label also gives weights and values of quarter, half and 1 moydore pieces, half pistoles, 1 pistoles and double pistoles, French Louis d'Or and half Louis and five sizes of Port Pieces. It dates between 1737 and approximately 1740 and has the recesses for scales and weights gouged out of the solid. Later cases of this type (about 1740–80) were made with dovetailed corners and partitioned compartments.

An ingenious folding type of balance, which obviated loose weights and was small enough to fit the pocket, became fashionable in the eighteenth century. Made of brass except for the pins which were steel, this pattern was designed for a limited range of coins and made by numerous makers. It was almost invariably fixed into a case hollowed from a block of solid Spanish mahogany, approximately $5\frac{1}{2}$ in. long by $\frac{7}{8}$ in. by $\frac{5}{8}$ in. Two examples, one open, the other closed, are left of PLATE 68. The scales are so devised that they open automatically with the case and fold flat as it is closed. On the end of the beam opposite to the scales pan is a pivoted weight, or "turn" as it is described, which swings outwards to weigh guineas and inwards to weigh half guineas. Perfection of detail is such that the cross pin, on to which the beam end drops, is covered with fine silk. On the other half of the beam the travelling slide registers under or over weights. The original instruction label is in the box and bears the name of the maker, "Bell of Prescot, Lancashire". The case shown closed contains similar scales, except that they are for sovereigns and half-sovereigns and were made by "Steven Houghton of Ormskirk" about 1770.

A pair of nineteenth-century apothecary's scales, on mahogany base with drawer, is in PLATE 69.

MISCELLANEOUS—In PLATE 69 are also several other interesting devices. Left is a boxwood microscope of about 1780. The trumpet-shaped instrument adjacent is a typical nineteenth-century ebony stethoscope. These are also to be found made of cedar and boxwood. Some of the best have ivory ear discs or bases, with a ring of ivory forming a rim to the "trumpet". Some were made to fold and wedge in the doctor's silk hat. All are wooden modifications of the paper roll devised by Rene Laennec in 1819. The bi-aural type superseded them about 1886.

Extreme right (69) is an eighteenth-century apothecary's chopping board for medicinal roots and herbs. It has a curious chopper, the blade being shaped to resemble a horse.

Thermometers, which date from Galileo's discovery in 1592, provide interesting treen cases and holders; early specimens are rare.

MORTARS—Mortars for crushing and grinding spices, snuff, almonds, coffee, candy, ginger and other roots must be among the earliest devices used by man. The Book of Proverbs (xxvii. 22) says: "Though thou shouldest bray [beat small] a fool in a mortar among wheat with a pestle, yet will not his foolishness depart from him". In the middle ages, the curious custom arose of parading certain offenders against the law with mortars hung round their necks and accompanied by a bell ringer.

Until the late seventeenth century, mortars seem to have been made from almost any wood and in very varied shapes. A selection is in PLATE 70. Their only common characteristics were thick walls and bases. Large domestic and trade mortars were and very often are of stone, particularly marble. A number of fine sixteenth-century bronze and bell metal mortars exist. From the seventeenth century English mortars in all sizes were mostly made from lignum vitæ and were well finished. One of this wood, dating from the early eighteenth century, is left of PLATE 70. It measures $8\frac{1}{2}$ in. both in diameter and height and is typical of Georgian design. Next is an ancient and curious specimen, which shows traces of a lacquered pattern of stamped noughts and crosses. Neither its date nor country of origin is known. The equally crude beech octagonal mortar of font-like form has considerable age, but there is no way of dating it. It has been used for crushing salt. Extreme right, the example with close-fitting pestle next to it, is country made.

The two small lignum mortars in front are early eighteenth-century apothecary's mortars, as is the unusually decorated specimen (69).

*   *   *

COLLECTORS NOTES

An early seventeenth-century walnut and ivory ell rule, very similar to that illustrated and described but of rectangular section, is in the Wallace Collection. A draper's yard measure is in Cheltenham Museum and the early microscope, stethoscope, etc. (69), are in the Rev. C. J. Sharp's Museum, Shepreth.

Cardiff Museum has a large and varied array of tally sticks, including those in PLATE 66. Tally sticks from the twelfth century onwards are to be seen in the Museum of the Public Record Office, Chancery Lane. Rye and District Museum has hop tallies; Hove Museum has an abacus.

The Science Museum, South Kensington, in addition to displaying tally sticks and abacus, shows a comprehensive collection depicting the progress of scientific calculation, including in many instances the inventors' original models, largely of wood. These include "Napier's bones", Gaspard Schott's cylinders, Gunter's seventeenth-century slide rule and Mannheim's improved version of 1850, as well as an unusual cylindrical rule of boxwood, designed about 1870 for calculating ballistics. Other interesting wooden measuring devices exhibited include an early nineteenth-century fine German ell rod of mahogany with sycamore inlays and showing early use of the metric system. There is also Davis' quadrant of 1590 for observing the sun's altitude and several seventeenth- and eighteenth-century nocturnals—astronomical instruments for taking observations to ascertain the hour of the night; one of them, dated 1702, is a fine boxwood example.

Also in this museum is an "octant" made by Benjamin Martin (1750). It is mounted on a well proportioned Georgian mahogany cabriole tripod and is expressive of the complete domination even of scientific instruments by the prevailing style in cabinet making. Numerous barometers also reflect, in their cases, changing furniture fashions. Weighing machines and balances are well represented and include examples of "bismars".

Among the exhibits are several "perambulators"—not our "prams", but early nineteenth-century measuring wheels of known circumference, which, when trundled along the ground, operate a recording mechanism. There is also an interesting eighteenth-century levelling rod.

The history of microscopes is told by original models dating from 1680. The early ones are mostly partially treen.

Early weights and scales, including Roman and Greek specimens, are in the British Museum. Hull Museum has a collection of over 200 money scales and weights. The National Museum of Wales, Cardiff, and Colchester Museum have good selections.

Messrs. W. T. Avery, Ltd., of Soho Foundry, Birmingham, have a unique museum devoted to weighing equipment dating from 2500 B.C. onwards. It can be viewed on application. A comprehensive history of weighing by the late Mr. Benton is contained in twenty-two illustrated volumes entitled *The Record of Avery Historical Museum*. A copy is in the Science Museum Library.

A seventeenth-century weighing set of Dutch origin, somewhat resembling the diamond merchant's scales illustrated, is in the National Museum of Antiquities, Edinburgh. The Victoria and Albert Museum has several fine seventeenth-century sets.

In Mr. and Mrs. J. F. Parker's private Folk Museum at Tickenhill Manor, Bewdley, is a 49 in. dip stick, calibrated in Imperial gallons and a wooden hydrometer.

Commander F. Hart, R.N. (Retd.), has, in his private collection at Chipping Campden, a finely made and unusual pocket sundial of pearwood, 6 in. in diameter, dated 1694.

72　*Etuis*, woolwinders, wool bowls and silk thrower

73　Scissors case, revolving reel stand, wool bowl and *etuis*

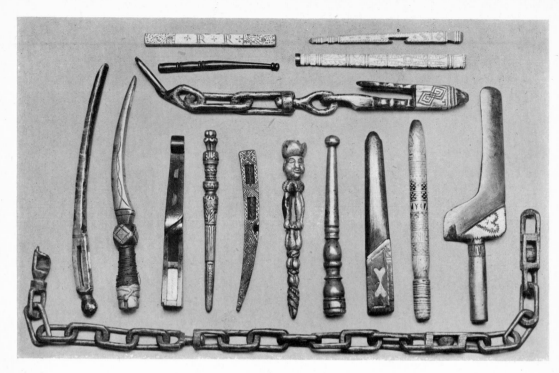

74   A selection of knitting sheaths

75   Further selection of knitting sheaths

PART NINE

STITCHCRAFT AND TEXTILES

THIS chapter commenced with Eve, for ever since her day wood has played a continuous but changing part in textile manufacture, until, by a complex process, we now obtain from it lustrous silk-like fibres nearly equalling those achieved by humble silkworms aided by mulberry trees.

Records show that silkworm culture existed in China nearly 4,500 years ago. The secret was well guarded for not until about 1,500 years ago were silkworms reported in India, reputed smuggled by a Chinese princess who married the ruler of Khotan. Raw silk reached Constantinople at the beginning of the sixth century but, according to most authorities, it was the sixteenth before silkworm breeding, travelling via Spain and Italy, was established in France and another century before it became an English in-dustry, largely due to encouragement by the Stuarts. This seems debatable for, in the fourteenth century, an English Act was passed forbidding importation of silken thread and manufactured goods. Its object was "to protect certain old established silk women against Lombards and Italians, who brought such quantities of silk threads and rebands [ribbons] into the country that the established native throwsters were impoverished". A throwster is one who "throws" silk, silk throwing being a process of twisting the very fine thread taken from the cocoon after its death by immersion in hot water. A rare old silk thrower, the device formerly used in silk throwing, is in the foreground of PLATE 72. The recent history of this example was related in the Introduction. As originally used, the silk threads were passed over the four notches in the crossbar. When six threads were operated, this bar was replaced by one with six notches, and so on. The slot in the lower portion takes a fixed hardwood bar, which holds the device vertical, but not rigidly so; thus, if any silk threads became knotted and tension were exerted, some play was allowed, preventing the silk from breakage. Formerly threads, after leaving the arm, were twisted on a wheel; now the operation is executed mechanically.

Not only the silkworm faces competition from substitutes from wood; even sheep have competition from wood cellulose wool now.

Formerly wood was only used for the implements for textile making. In the long, dark evenings and winter days of northern climes, when scattered communities had to be self sufficient, the men made wooden appliances which the women employed for carding, spinning and weaving cloth, linen and blankets and for sewing, knitting and lacemaking. Although spinning had been invented by the Bronze Age, spinning wheels did not entirely supersede spindles in England until the early sixteenth century and in many countries, including some in Europe, the older spindle and hand distaff are still used extensively.

DISTAFFS AND SPINNING WHEELS—Preliminaries to wool spinning were and still are fleecing, scouring, washing and dying. Then came carding, which employed the first treen device, the carding implement, for preparing the wool lengthwise, as far as possible, into delicate rope-like forms called "continuous rovings", which were fixed on the distaff.

Flax, when gathered, was freed from seed pods, macerated and dressed. It was then "scutched" to free the broken flax from the boon or stalk. This part of the process employed a scutching block and wooden scutching knife to strike the boon from the flax. In North-West Europe these scutching knives were extremely decorative, being gaily coloured and elaborately carved, as were also the "temples" used for stretching the web.

After "scutching", flax was hackled or further dressed with a flax comb or "gill", as Parson Woodforde terms it in his diary (1788). It then went on the distaff and thence the wool or flax was pulled out for spinning on hand spindle or wheel.

Distaffs, particularly in North-West Europe, were often elaborately carved love tokens—possibly with an ulterior motive attached to the love! They were designed for three different modes of use. In their oldest form used conjointly with a spindle, they were hand staffs, held under the left arm, the roving being twisted spirally by the right hand of the worker, who could walk about while spinning. Used as separate accessories of spinning wheels, distaffs were sometimes floor stands, which might terminate at the top in a crown, as in the Scandinavian model (126), or they might have simply turned stems, finishing in a knop or tapering to a point at top, with loops hanging down. In such cases, the roving was slung through the loop and the distaff was often part of the spinning wheel. By 1780–90 the wheels, which had been a feature of most homes in the British Isles for at least 300 years, spinning laboriously one thread at a time, were falling into disuse. This was due first to Hargreave's invention of 1767 of the "Spinning Jenny" (named after his wife), which could spin 120 threads at once, Arkwright's water frame of about 1775 and Crompton's "mule" of 1774, so called because of its intermediate position between the other two inventions.

The next stage in cloth making took place on a hand loom, which device, incidentally, was used in Egypt many thousand years before the days of power machines. It is interesting that the name "Webster", common as a surname, originally denoted a male weaver. The only thing connected with the crossing and interlacing of "warp" and "weft", which the treen collector can include, is a shuttle. Turned wood ancillaries of spinning are spools, bobbins and reels, which take us to reel stands.

REEL STANDS—The yew wood example (73), with each gallery revolving independently, was to be found a century ago on the village shop counter. It was made in various sizes.

EMBROIDERY FRAMES—Embroidery has developed its special but uninteresting wooden table clamps and floor standing double frames, or hoops of various hardwoods. Pictorial embroidery and even painted textiles are often incorrectly called tapestry but tapestry, whether of wool or silk, was originally essentially a woven product of the loom, first made at Arras and consequently often called by that name.

WINDERS—The need for winding threads from skein to ball has produced many weird and wonderful wooden gadgets as substitutes for a husband's out-stretched arms. The most common, also in pairs, were the many variants of the table clamping wheels (top, 72). Some have additions on top, such as a thimble holder, pincushion or shallow dish or spike for holding the ball. The small rosewood examples are Victorian; the larger ones are eighteenth century. The large olivewood revolving winder is a simple form of the various umbrella-frame contraptions, used by our Georgian ancestors; it is well constructed and effective, designed to be folded when idle.

NEEDLECASES—The *étuis* or needle cases in the same picture are English standing patterns of horn. Two Swiss carved wood examples and an English acorn-shaped one are in PLATE 73, and two peasant decorated travelling-cases and a cornet-shaped needle and thread case in PLATE 107.

KNITTING SHEATHS—Knitting, originally called netting, developed another and more interesting wooden device than the treen knitting needle, formerly called a "prick". This was the knitting sheath or stick, into which the needle was stuck.

The words knitting, netting, knotting and knoetting seem synonymous and these terms, applied to knitting as we know it, date from Saxon times. Shakespeare makes several references to knitting. Queen Elizabeth was presented by her silk woman, Mrs. Montague, with a pair of silk stockings and thereafter never wore cloth. Henry VIII is known to have worn Spanish silk stockings on occasion and a tradition lingers in the Shetlands that knitting was introduced there by sailors rescued from a wreck of the Armada. The Scots, on the other hand, claim that they invented knitting, basing their claim on Saint Fiacre, the son of a Scottish king, being chosen as the patron saint of a guild of French stocking knitters in Paris, about the year 1527.

Stocking frame knitting was introduced about 1589 by William Lee of Nottinghamshire and the mechanical principles of his invention have remained almost unaltered. His invention increased the speed from about 100 stitches per minute to 1,000 or more on the frame. No invention, however, has lessened the popularity of hand-knitting and throughout the eighteenth and nineteenth centuries and possibly considerably earlier, knitting sheaths were used commonly in Scotland, in the border counties of England and Scotland and in Wales. During the winter months, friends in the dales met at one another's houses in turn and held what they called a "knitting go forth", at which the knitters sat round a fire, while one member narrated tales. Knitting sheaths never seem to have penetrated far south into England, as distinct from Wales, but knitting itself never gained the same popularity, although Celia Fiennes, touring East Anglia in 1698, remarked on "the ordinary people knitting 4 or 5 in a company under the hedges". Robert Southey immortalised Dent in Yorkshire as the village of dreadful knitters and Henry Brougham, during his election address in Ravenstonedale in 1820, remarked that the name of the place should be changed to Knittingdale.

Knitting sheaths were made in considerable variety and pierced to a depth varying between 1 and $2\frac{1}{2}$ in.; they were worn on the right side, in order to release the fingers of the right hand for "throwing" the worsted and to support the weight of the knitting. They were notched on the apron strings, or more often carried by a belt, rudely called a cow-band and, as shown in PLATE 74 and PLATE 75, some were designed with an "eye" or slot for threading on the band, some with a notch to clip on, some to sew on and some to tuck in the band. Those with a diagonal groove were for fitting on crossed apron strings. A hook, usually metal, called a clew holder, was also attached to the cow-band to hold the ball of yarn, called a clew, or to support the knitting.

The oldest dated knitting sheath which I have seen is carved with the date 1680 and the initial "T". It is lying across PLATE 74, third line from the top and is doubly rare because its clew holder and wooden chain are carved from the same piece as the sheath.

The first vertical sheath (left, same plate) is eighteenth century and is bone, as is also the right one in the second horizontal row. All the others are wood. These sheaths usually vary between 5 and 10 in. in length and like distaffs in Scandinavia, spoons in Wales and lace bobbins in England, were often made as love tokens. The eighth from the left, which is mahogany, clearly shows joined hearts in inlay, whilst the goosewing pattern sheath (extreme right) is carved with a heart. Next is one carved with initials "F.R.", date 1753 and is inlaid with black and red composition. Second on the left, the gift of a sailor, is carved with initials "L" and "M" and its handle bound with cord and wire which, with chamfered central knop, strongly resembles some handles of sailmaker's liners in PLATE 113. Still from the left, the third is inlaid mahogany, terminating in a violin scroll, with the name "Ann Gray" in the "window"; the fourth, probably French, is elaborately carved, though much worn. The fifth is finely chip carved all over, curved and bears initials "FR" and "BP" and has two windows. Next is another nautical one, amusingly carved with a corpulent ship's captain above four stems bound with rope; it is apparently plane wood, not later than 1720, but may be seventeenth century. The seventh (left) is eighteenth-century turning. The two rectangular section boxwood sheaths (top row) are both eighteenth century, chip carved. The one on the left, with the initials "RR", is pierced at both ends.

The wooden chain which completes this picture is not a knitting accessory, but a pathetic relic which will recall recent sad memories to many. Carved by a French prisoner in England during the Napoleonic wars, it is out of a single piece of wood 29 in. long and includes a revolving link, two balls and lanterns and a clenched hand. One wonders how many months each link commemorated.

PLATE 75 shows another fine selection. Right, is a scroll or violin pattern of split type for fitting over a belt and is English or Welsh, of chip carved rosewood, late eighteenth or early nineteenth century. It was two "windows"; one contains a plait of hair, the other the initials "E.T." The second is walnut, eighteenth century; it is carved with initials "J.B." or "I.B." The third, of finely carved boxwood, is dated 1726 and has a finely executed figure above lantern and ball; the threaded base is possibly for an extension to take a clew holder. The fourth, the scimitar pattern, is fruitwood. The fifth, mahogany, is a good example of the fish pattern—doubtless a nineteenth-century sailor's gift. The sixth (above No. 5) is most unusual; the fossil worm pattern is carved boxwood. The seventh, another scimitar shape, is walnut, chip carved in floral scrolls. The eighth, probably Welsh, is chip carved sycamore, with a belt loop, double heart emblem inlaid with bone and a plaque bearing the inscription "A.M. Juli 25th 1816". Second left is a small English or Welsh chip carved sheath with ball and lantern and an open belt loop and ring for the clew holder. It is carved with hearts, the name "SUSAN WHITE", the date 1792 and initials "T.H.", presumably those of the donor. Extreme left is a cleanly finished, open scroll type sheath, with groove for fitting over the belt. The scroll face is carved with roses, one side with an ear of corn and the reverse with a thistle and other flowers; on the scroll back is carved "MARY ANN HEDLEY".

The Italian, seventeenth-century boxwood knitting stick (77), to which reference is made in the Introduction, is in a class apart as a carving, but unsuitable as an article of everyday use. It is $11\frac{1}{2}$ in. long and the fine, intricate carving includes numerous scrolls and rings, on one of which a dolphin, balanced on his tail, holds in his mouth the base of a pedestal; on this stands a muscular little putto, balancing on his head a lofty structure of formal foliage and flowers.

WOOL HOLDERS—Controlling the ball of wool seems always to have worried knitters and it must have caused particular concern when the only illuminant was rush, candle or firelight. Reference has been made already to clew holders and in the seventeenth and eighteenth centuries various other expedients were adopted. One was the windpipe of a goose, in which some dried peas were inserted and the pipe then bent into a circle to act as a foundation for the clew which, when dropped, betrayed its whereabouts by rattling. Another device, called a "broach", was simply a piece of wood, broad at one end, for inserting in the knitter's shoe, the other end forming a wooden pin to hold the clew. The simplest and most effective was the Georgian wool bowl and it was so good that it is surprising that it has disappeared. I have given several to ladies, who now use them invariably. Two are in PLATE 72 and one, slightly different, containing knitting, is right of PLATE 73. These bowls seem always to have been of lignum vitæ, because of its weight and they are smooth, well polished and curved inside in a perfect segment, sufficiently deep to prevent the ball "jumping" and with a rounded rim which allows the wool to unwind without jamming, as knitting proceeds. A larger bowl, usually $5\frac{1}{4}$ in. in diameter, fitted with a central circular pillar, was used for coarse wool.

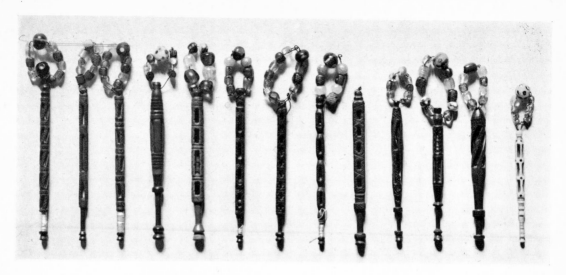

76 "Church window" and "mother-in-babe" lace bobbins

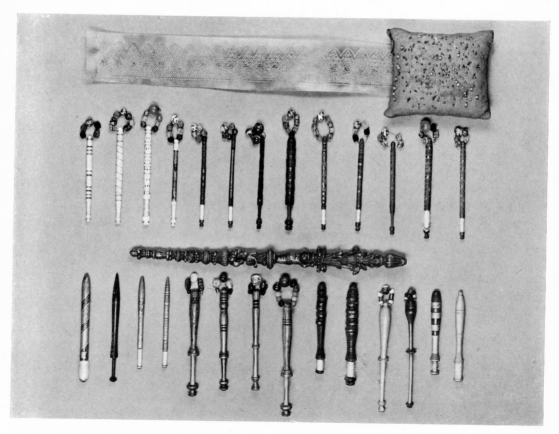

77 A selection of "Tiger," "Leopard," "bitted" and other bobbins, a lace pattern and pincushion with hand-made pins, and a finely carved knitting sheath

79   Russian flower vase, Swiss urns and Norwegian carved bowl

78   Home adornment from the Orient

supplement under the heading of Lathes, particularly page 166, and *Watches*, by G. H. Baillie (1929), page 223.

For engine turning high skill, a steady hand, infinite patience and good eyesight are as essential qualities as the right material. Only the densest woods can be used, for the technique is really that of the ivory or metal worker and the work in wood can be as fine and the effect even more handsome, owing to grain and colour variations. To appreciate the perfection of this work, it must be remembered that all these examples were made before the days of automatic lathes and modern illuminants and that one false move spelt ruin. Ebony, cocos and rosewood were the woods favoured for all the examples in PLATE 84, except one circular snuff box, which is lignum vitæ. Clever use has been made in this box of the light colour to "frame" the engine turned heartwood, the frame being left boldly curved and plain, owing to the chippiness of lignum. The eighteenth-century ebony urn, with pedestal and ivory ring, possesses great dignity and superb detail. The open cup on stem, the small cup with cover next to it and the ring-stand (right) especially are miniature monuments to their skilful and patient creators. The mahogany bowl (back, 4), the oval tobacco box (56) and one string box (63) are other good examples. One wonders whether they were made by men of leisure as a hobby, by sweated labour in order to live, or by artistic men of skill, encouraged by the patrons of the golden age of craftsmanship.

ADORNMENT FOR THE PERSON—The fig tree seems to have provided the first personal adornment and ever since, various trees have provided apparel and adornment for a large proportion of mankind. After fig leaves came woven bark cloth and this, in a wide range of simple designs, some possessing certain artistic merit, still supplies the clothing needs of the inhabitants of many lands.

A particularly interesting and early example of treen, which appears to be a girdle intended for personal adornment, is illustrated in PLATE 83. Believed to be of thorn wood, this fourteenth-century, French chain is in exceptional condition. In design and quality of workmanship it is an excellent example of fine, small scale mediæval wood carving, comparing favourably with the work of any later age. The chain, apparently cut from a single piece of wood, 54 in. long, has each of its twenty-three separate double links carved along the edges and exquisitely ornamented with a different central subject on each face. I understand that an account of this and related objects is in preparation by Mr. W. A. Thorpe.

"Busk" occurs in English sixteenth-century literature as a verb meaning "to dress" or "prepare" and the term "busked" is sometimes used instead of "attired", but the word "busk" has also been applied to whalebone, steel or wooden stiffeners for corsets for many centuries. Most busks were purely utilitarian and not intended for view, but the fashions of 1670–80 and of 1785–90 both decreed a form of bustle or crinoline for women. To accentuate the fullness at the hips, the corsage was long and wasp waisted, descending to a deep "V" in front and this created a fashion for long busks. In rustic circles, these busks were adorned with carving and presented as love tokens for insertion in the corsage. I have only seen one carved busk of the seventeenth century and, apart from one dated 1749, all the others which I have examined date between 1777 and 1799. The fashions appear to have been short-lived, which is not surprising considering how uncomfortable wearers must have found busks 14 or 15 in. long, of unyielding wood or whalebone. Good specimens are now extremely rare. They were mostly collected together by the late Dr. Oxford and from him they passed to the late Owen Evan-Thomas, whose collection was sold at Sotheby's in 1946.

Of those in PLATE 85, the first left is sycamore, with chip carved border enclosing a double heart, the initials "S.I." and "I.I." and date 1798. The second includes a finely carved roundel centre motif, a heart at top and initials "M.H." on the reverse. The third is exceptionally finely carved with roundels, diamonds, hearts and wheels. It is dated 1777 and 1781 on the back. The fourth, inlaid in bone with fishes, birds, snakes, hearts and wheels, is dated 1787 and was doubtless a sailor's gift. The fifth is dagger-shaped and has a crudely carved diamond pattern, with a heart, sun, stars and birds in front and at the back the initials "A.B." The sixth is a fine sycamore (?) carving; the top is heart-shaped, with sun and stars below and intertwined heart motifs. The seventh, a well-worn sycamore busk, has a centre motif of double hearts.

In PLATE 86 are four more busks, all chip carved with prominent heart motifs and all dating between 1782 and 1786.

Small hand mirrors and fans both have a long history of coquetry. In their heyday, they spoke a recognised language and their subtle movements conveyed many a message of hope or discouragement. When the wielder of the fan could also study herself in the mirror simultaneously, the result must often have proved irresistible. Henri III of France set the seal of fashion of fans towards the end of the sixteenth century and Queen Elizabeth imported large quantities and was considered their godmother in England. Fans containing mirrors were popular in the eighteenth and nineteenth centuries and three nineteenth-century, Italian examples, in olivewood cases, are in PLATE 80. One is open and the two which are closed show their back and front respectively. Pull the top tassel and the fan opens; pull the lower one and it shuts and is ready to suspend from the wrist. In PLATE 86 are an Indian fan with carved handles and pierced blades, a fan made from Seychelles palm leaves and a fixed wooden fan, in the Oriental taste, made in the Tunbridge district by Italian labour between 1850–70. In this example the light background shows the natural grain of the wood.

In PLATE 87 are three handbag mirrors; the two with handles are inlaid Sheraton specimens; the larger is the rarer, containing a convex magnifying mirror. The mirror in case with lid is early nineteenth century. Inside the other necklace are three wooden scent flasks, interesting as examples of three fashions of three countries, three centuries and three materials. The small circular German pocket flask, with centre medallion carved with a basket of flowers on one face, a "trophy" of musical instruments on reverse and border of flowers, is made from coquilla nut and is typical of German "Biedermeier" design of 1820. The crude, eighteenth-century, Swedish flask is hollowed out of a burry root, bone studded and silver mounted. The late seventeenth- or early eighteenth-century Italian flask is in a class apart, being beautifully carved from a boxwood block and finely ornamented with acanthus scrolls, scenes and oval lozenges containing classical heads. Another finely carved eighteenth-century boxwood scent flask, probably French, is in front of PLATE 80.

At the bottom of the photograph is a great rarity: a pair of Georgian wooden shoe buckles, with fine steel inner frames and prongs. These buckles, a type familiar in silver, are beautifully made, the double curves being built up of four cross layers of sawn cut veneers, glued together as in modern plywood. The edges are painted to protect them. The double curve of the face layer is a particularly remarkable piece of work, consisting of a centre cross banding of boxwood, inlaid with pin points alternately of ebony and mahogany (?) and edged on each side with stringings of ebony and satinwood, then cross bandings of kingwood and finally another stringing of satinwood. The total width of these nine veneer strips is only $\frac{1}{2}$ in. The width of the buckles is $2\frac{3}{4}$ in., their length $4\frac{5}{8}$ in.

Nineteenth-century adornment occupies the rest of PLATE 87. The six carved buttons are walnut, the left necklace grey sycamore and the right boxwood. The tiny

80   Elaborate Swiss urn, " scuttle" box, Australian Mulga vase, carved dog-box, boxwood scent
flask, Victorian quizzing fans

81   Coquilla nut urns, vase and flask

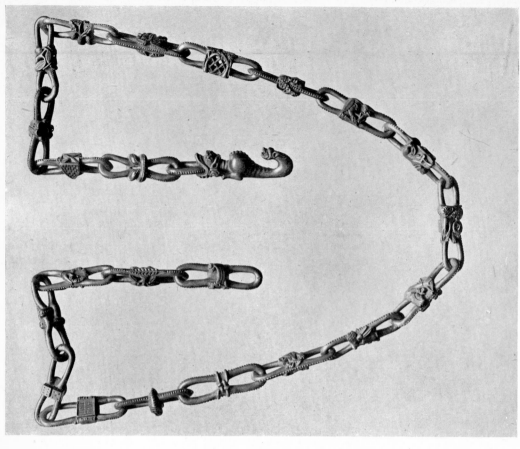

83 A superb 14th century, French chain girdle of thornwood, every link carved in a different pattern

82 Swiss urn, lignum vitæ vase, classically draped urn and delicately pierced cylinder

Victorian purse, 2 by $1\frac{1}{2}$ in., is of finely carved and pierced coquilla nut and contains two compartments lined with red satin.

In PLATES 88 to 90 we move to the Orient. For many centuries the Chinese have been famous for their fine work, particularly intricately carved wood, ivory, jade and lacquers. No larger than many precious stones and, in fact, used in place of jewels, the Chinese carvings in PLATE 89 and PLATE 90 are real masterpieces. It is difficult to imagine how they are ever created; to see them in detail requires a powerful magnifying glass.

Some of these miniature carvings are executed on canarium nuts, which are pierced through and through until they attain a lacey quality. Others embrace a city scene, with buildings and crowds, in the compass of half a peach stone.

Left of PLATE 88 is a whole canarium nut, with an overall length of $1\frac{1}{2}$ in. and a diameter of $\frac{7}{8}$ in. None of the carvings exceeds $1\frac{7}{16}$ in. by $\frac{13}{16}$ in. The other examples show some of the simplest forms. Left to right, the first is an ape-like figure, squatting on its haunches, with a smaller ape peeping over its head. Next is a tortoise walking over a pierced structure of intertwined leaves. The third is a conch shell; unfortunately it rolled over while being photographed and so missed showing on the reverse a Chinese gnome (or whatever similar creatures of that nationality are called) emerging from its shell. The fourth is some kind of oriental crustacean and extreme right is an ivory-tailed mouse. All these come under the heading of comparatively crude work.

In PLATE 89 are examples of finer work, varied deliberately for comparison. All are canarium nut carvings, approximately $\frac{5}{16}$ in. in diameter.

The nuts at the sides are intended as pendants and the centre one, with threaded base, was probably a stopper for a perfume flask. The threepenny piece is included for comparison of size. The left pendant portrays a house, before which is a mother rocking a cradle containing her baby. The right pendant shows a spreading tree, under which a man, with child on lap, is seated in a wheeled carriage drawn by a horseman. The scene on the reverse shows a man at an upper window, plucking blooms from a climbing plant, whilst below two musicians are playing cymbals. The grotesque seated figure on the flask stopper is bare chested, with ribs showing clearly. He is in a wicker carriage with two large wheels at the rear and two small ones at the sides. In his left hand he holds, bunched up, the reins of two miniature horsemen, who look hard-pressed in pulling him. Presumably horses and horsemen are shown smaller than the passenger to accentuate their menial position.

In PLATE 90 all are half-fruit stones, even finer than the previous carvings. The side specimens are probably intended as brooches and consist of most exquisitely carved sprays of roses, paper thick, so undercut and in such high relief that they are practically free standing. They measure $1\frac{7}{16}$ in. by $\frac{7}{8}$ in. wide. The centre example, taken from a bracelet, shows a scene with trees and a house in the background. In the right-hand foreground a merchant displays a jar and casket to three others seated at a carved table. In my collection is a complete bracelet of carved peach stones, showing varied and natural street scenes and mounted in gilt.

*　　　*　　　*

COLLECTORS NOTES

Examples of the type of treen described in this chapter are found scattered in nearly all museums. Stay busks are well represented in the Rev. C. J. Sharp's Museum, Shepreth; there are also specimens in the Buckinghamshire County Museum, Aylesbury. In the Victoria and Albert Museum is a boxwood stay busk dated 1675 and inscribed: WONE · A · QUISCHON · I · WAS · ASKED · WHICH · MAD · ME · RETURN · THESE · ANSURS · THAT · ISAAC · LOVEED · RABEKAH · HIS · WIFE · AND · WHY · MAY · I · NOT · LOVE · FRANSES.

PART ELEVEN

IN THE BEDCHAMBER

THE bedchamber and bed appeared in wealthy homes at the height of Egyptian, Grecian and Roman civilisations. All have left pictures or examples, but probably during most of the history of mankind the great majority slept wrapped in rugs or skins, on straw or rush-strewn floors.

Although in earlier times the wealthier monastries had "cells" and guest chambers and kings their bedchambers, it was not until the thirteenth century in England that even large manor houses began to offer privacy and then only the "solar" or combined bed-sitting and with-drawing room, in which the lord and lady of the manor performed their toilets, slept and received their guests, who, unless very important, still slept on the floor in the great hall. It was not until late in the fifteenth century that bedrooms became usual even in large houses. For 200 years after, the fashion of planning upper floors of great houses as continuous suites, the rooms of which formed corridors, must have made necessary the completely curtained beds which were customary. In smaller homes, beds were built into wall recesses of living rooms and curtained off or enclosed by doors during the day, as they still are in primitive parts and northern climes.

Some say that the bed wagon, with ashwood hoops and beech spars, enclosing a pan of charcoal in an iron trivet (91), was the predecessor of the charcoal-filled warming pan, but I doubt this and think that it was essentially an alternative eighteenth-century device, intended as an airer of beds that had been disused, rather than a bed warmer. The warming pan in England goes back to the sixteenth century, if not earlier, and I have never seen a bed wagon the construction of which could rightly claim such antiquity.

Whilst the impedimenta of the toilet was well advanced in wealthy homes in sixteenth-century England, it was left to the seventeenth to design the specialised dressing table.

Until the second half of the seventeenth century, the mirror was an imported rarity, usually small and only suitable for hand use. When manufacture began at Vauxhall, wall mirrors became fashionable, hung over tables, and late in the seventeenth century pivot mounting commenced, on a stand which often contained fitted toilet boxes. In the eighteenth century the mirror became an integral part of a small dressing table or chest, which was often ingeniously and elaborately fitted with boxes and compartments and made *en suite* with a minute washing or so-called powdering stand.

These articles of furniture and the treen which accompanied them were used equally by both sexes. Eighteenth-century young men of fashion were ridiculous coxcombs. A writer in the *Connoisseur* of April, 1755, describes a young man's dressing table as follows:

> "I could not but observe a number of boxes of different sizes, I had the curiosity to examine the contents of several, in one I found a lip-salve, in another a roll of pig-tail, in the middle stood a bottle of Eau de Luce, and a roll of perfumed pomatum, almond pastes and powder puffs. But I could not conceive for what use a small ivory comb could be designed, till the valet informed me it was a comb for the eyebrows."

COMBS—A fine boxwood comb of this type is in PLATE 93, together with a coarser wood comb, probably Scandinavian. John Evelyn, in *Sylva* (1670), refers to the use of boxwood for combs, quoting:

> *"Box-combs bear no small part*
> *In the Militia of the Female Art;*
> *They tye the Links which hold our Gallants fast*
> *And spread the nets to which fond Lovers hast."*

84   Examples of engine turning

85   Carved stay busks of the late 18th century

86   Fans and stay busks

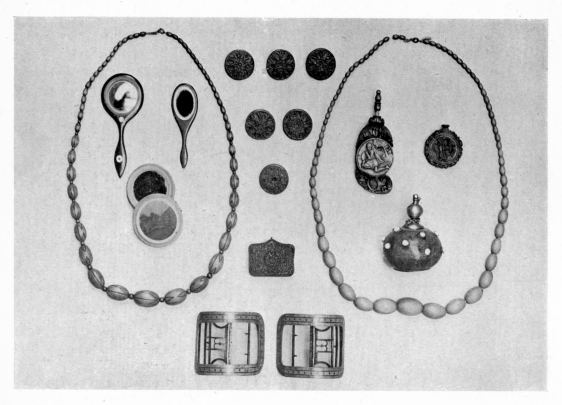

87   Adornment for the person. The scrolled boxwood scent flask and the Georgian inlaid
shoe buckles are of fine quality

88   A whole canarium nut and simply carved specimens

89   Chinese carved canarium nut pendants and flask stopper

90   Chinese carved peach stone brooches

91   18th century bed wagon

92   Wig stand, pin cushions, glove powdering flasks, razor case, toilet boxes and pots,
ring stands and button hook

H-form double combs were made throughout the Middle Ages. Considerable numbers of ivory and a few boxwood have survived. The example in PLATE 2 was formerly in the collection of Philip Howard, Esq., of Corby Castle, and was exhibited at the Art Treasures Exhibition. Such combs are generally known as liturgical combs, but it is too sweeping a generalisation to label all thus. Indubitably combs were recognised liturgical accessories, for combing the episcopal locks at the consecration of bishops, and they were used in the Coronation ceremonial, but the subjects depicted on many show that they were the normal secular combs of the wealthy in mediæval times. Like mirror cases, they formed part of the fitting of "trousses" or dressing cases, which are recorded in old inventories. Documents also exist which name some of the comb makers and the mercers who sold them. In a tapestry exhibited recently at the Victoria and Albert Museum, a harlot was depicted using a double comb.

Love scenes form the most popular carved ornament of H-combs and doubtless many of these beautiful works were love tokens. The magnificent example illustrated, probably dating from the late fifteenth century, has in the centre panel a clenched hand holding an arrow, which is about to pierce a heart. The owner of the hand is also careful to indicate that he wears his heart upon his sleeve. The other panels have been recessed, lined with silk and inlaid with bone or ivory fretted ornament, which suggests a Mediterranean origin for this comb. On the reverse, the centre panel consists of strapwork, reminiscent of the borders of fifteenth-century illuminated manuscripts. The side panels resemble those illustrated.

Even when of wood, the fine tools used and the technique employed in manufacture were those of the ivory worker. In tenth- and eleventh-century combs, the H is taller than it is broad, but later specimens reverse these proportions.

DRESSING TABLE TREEN—In PLATE 92 is a selection of pincushions, trinket stands and powder boxes, etc., mostly nineteenth century. The two lignum vitæ pincushion stands (back row) are carved in basketware design, unfortunately only too fashionable in late Victorian days. Whilst not inappropriate as a pincushion stand, it looks ridiculous in some cases, such, for instance, as the inkwells (64). Beside the pincushions is a powder box of 1780, with original design in faded red and blue on a white painted background. The box with trinket holder on top has a pincushion inside the lid. When elbow length gloves were worn, the two nineteenth-century glove powdering flasks were as essential adjuncts of the toilet table as the rosewood glove stretcher (right, 93). Glove powdering flasks with screw caps, for use when travelling, are in PLATE 106.

Gloves have great antiquity and played an important symbolic part in feudal days, the throwing down of a glove being the recognised form of challenge to a duel and the gift of a glove being an esteemed love token from a lady to her knight.

"Fruit" boxes are one of the charming eighteenth- and nineteenth-century fashions and are much sought by collectors. They occur as tea caddies, string boxes and toilet boxes. The realistically painted pear (left, 92) is a nineteenth-century bottle case; next, the boxwood apple is a powder box; the plum is beech and the small apples are burr birch and walnut respectively.

Three of the nineteenth-century ring stands are Tunbridgeware; that on the extreme right is walnut. In front, the three small pincushions, the rouge box (with glass liner) and the "patch" box are further dainty Tunbridgeware examples. The buttonhook, with handle in form of an amusing face, is skilfully carved from a nut. The crudely engraved razor case (extreme right), with pivoted action lid and sliding wooden catch, is hollowed from a solid block and is late seventeenth century.

PLATE 93 shows some more dressing-table treen. Left to right on the shelf are—a circular pin tray, made from Californian redwood burr; a modern stinkwood powder bowl from South Africa, the excellent design ruined, in my opinion, by the high gloss varnish invariably applied to these products; three late eighteenth- or early nineteenth-century rosewood toilet pots; another South African stinkwood bowl and a small syca-more bowl of the late seventeenth century, somewhat resembling a single handled quaich, but with inward curving rim. The latter is the kind of article the original use of which raises some doubt, but I think that it was a shaving bowl.

In front (right) are two unusual late eighteenth- or early nineteenth-century mahogany bottle cases. They were purchased in Worcester and as the only similar examples which I have seen are in Cheltenham Museum, they may be a West of England pattern.

MIRRORS—Metal mirrors were used by the ancients; silvered glass is believed to have originated in Italy in the fourteenth century and glass mirrors in use until the reign of Charles II came from there.

One of a pair of superb quality Italian Renaissance walnut mirror frames of the early sixteenth century is illustrated as the frame of the title page. Measuring 23 in. by $18\frac{1}{2}$ in., these frames, which comprise masterly compositions of delicate arabesques, are rendered more remarkable because each is carved from a single, unjointed block of walnut, glued on to a pine underframing and veneered on all edges. The remarkable state of preservation of these frames is due largely to vandalism, for when I purchased them the fine outlines of the delicate carvings were reduced to a series of slight undulations resulting from many excessive layers of paint. The top coat being white enamel and their contents cheap modern mirrors, the frames at first sight appeared to be Victorian moulded "composition" and but for the blurred outlines of the classical motifs, I should never have given them a second glance. Their stripping entailed many weeks of patient labour but the successful exposure of the fineness of the carving, the perfection of its design and the lovely bronze colour of the walnut were ample reward.

Another fine mirror frame, $9\frac{1}{2}$ in. by $8\frac{1}{2}$ in., oval, of carved, pierced and delicately undercut boxwood, is left of PLATE 93. It contains its original silvered plate. Although obviously owing much to Italian influence, this frame is believed to be of late eighteenth-century Portuguese origin.

In front are two Georgian hand-mirrors in Sheraton inlaid mahogany frames and above, in a circular ebony frame, is a small convex magnifying mirror, a type rare in the eighteenth century.

WIG STANDS AND POWDERING TUBES—Periwigs became fashionable for men at the Restoration and whether cause or effect, numerous close cropped "Roundheads" became "Cavaliers" overnight. The real reason for wearing wigs appears to have been the introduction of the French fashion of powdering. Pepys (May, 1662) tells of the impossibility of keeping his head clean with the greasing and powdering and his fears that he will be driven to wearing a "perriwig". By November, 1663, he had succumbed for he states: "Up to Church . . . and there I found my coming in a perriwig did not prove so strange to the world as I was afraid it would." In 1665 the Great Plague impeded the fashion, due to the fear, as Pepys relates, that hair for wigs might have been ". . . cut off the heads of people dead of the plague". The plague had no perma-nent affect, for by 1680 the fashion was so firmly established that the larger and better planned houses which followed the Great Fire, were built with powdering closets leading from the bedrooms. An additional one was often provided on half landings, where visiting gallants could use the three-legged wash-stands to "make up" and repowder their wigs, aided by the powder puff provided in the domed powder box above the

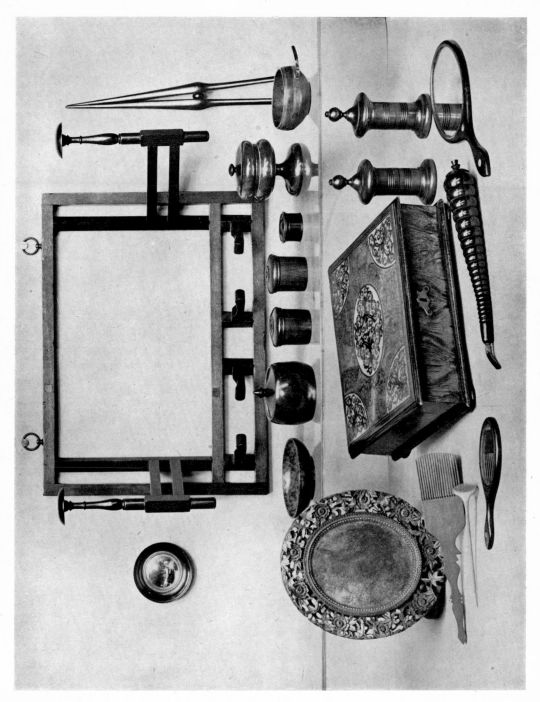

93 Miscellanea of the toilet

94   Miniature "grandfather" and architectural watch stands and 15th century jewel casket

95   Watchstands of the 18th and 19th centuries and early Victorian jewel casket

central drawer, which contained the "patch" boxes and perfumes. They then rinsed their hands in rosewater poured from the miniature ewer, at the base of the stand, into the equally minute basin at the top and were ready for presentation. Bickersteth (1768) refers satirically to the typical man of fashion as:

"A coxcomb, a fop, a dainty milk sop
Who, essenced, and dizen'd from bottom to top
Looks just like a doll for a milliner's shop.
A thing full of prate and pride and conceit;
All fashion, no weight;
Who shrugs and takes snuff and carries a muff;
A minnikin, finicking, French powder-puff."

The effeminate dress of the fashionable eighteenth-century man and time wasted in personal adornment formed the theme of numerous articles. The *Connoisseur* (1754) says:

"These male beauties will spend the whole morning scenting their linen, dressing their hair and arching their eyebrows. They have their toilettes too as well as the ladies, set out with washes, perfumes and cosmetics."

According to other references they obviously needed perfumes, as personal cleanliness played no part in fashion and both sexes used musk to an overpowering degree.

In smaller houses powdering was performed in bedrooms and men and women of fashion, wearing dust cloaks and with faces enclosed in stiff paper cones, like dunces' caps, sat while their wigs were pomaded, perfumed and powdered. When a powderer was employed, powder was blown on through a wood ringed powdering tube, shaped like a carrot, the stalk forming a mouthpiece and the root the spray nozzle. The specimen (front, 93), formerly in the Owen Evan-Thomas collection, is rosewood; the six smallest rings are flexible, mounted on leather, and a fine screen is inside the perforated nozzle. In some specimens a small bellows replaces the mouthpiece.

Men, during the wig-wearing fashion, had shaven heads and wore turbans or nightcaps when at home and not entertaining. The making and curling of wigs was carried out on miniature wooden heads, called wig blocks, made to stand or clamp to a table. Men of fashion were luckier than women, who had to sit for hours while their own hair, interwoven with artificial additions, was dressed over cushions of tow, which advanced in height and complexity with the years of the century. Finally, these mountains, which in their most exaggerated forms had their pinnacles crowned by artificial flowers, fruits, feathers, ribbons, birds in nests and even miniature windmills, ships and carriages, reached such a pitch that they necessitated women travelling in sedan chairs with open roofs and sleeping sitting up in bed! The structures were so expensive and tedious to erect that they were undisturbed for weeks on end and the need for head scratchers is understandable.

About 1785 powdering declined but as early as 1765 many young men of fashion commenced to abandon wigs and the periwig makers petitioned the King complaining that "men will wear their own hair". By 1789 the change of fashion had spread to the old, for then Parson Woodforde recorded: "I did not know old Mr. Dalton at first as he now wears his hair". By 1795, when a tax of one guinea per "head" was levied on powdered hair, all except lawyers, clergy and members of Parliament were wearing their own hair and these survivors soon became known as guinea-pigs.

Generally, in the eighteenth century, wig and bonnet stands, though varying in outlines of turnings, were interchangeable and followed the lines of the $12\frac{1}{2}$ in. high, simple mahogany example (left, 92). This one is fixed in height, but some are adjustable in similar manner to the candlestands (124). The "mushrooms" for the wigs and bonnets vary considerably in size, but there is no reason to believe that all large ones were intended for wigs and small ones for bonnets, or vice versa.

The mahogany wig stand, for suspension on a wall (back, 93) is a more unusual type. When closed it lies quite flat. The two pivoted "gates" swing out when required; below, four pivoted arms are provided for cravats. When I borrowed it from Mr. and Mrs. T. W. Bagshawe for photographing, I had never seen another of this type, but recently have come across three more. My wife found and purchased one of identical form, except that the frame, instead of being square section mahogany, is bobbin-turned fruitwood, while I have bought one like that illustrated and one with an oval back frame enclosing a needlework panel, two pivoted gates with mushrooms for wigs, but with four cravat pegs fixed permanently outwards. This latter specimen looks quite Victorian and may mark a transition between eighteenth-century wig stands and nineteenth-century bedroom "holders" designed for dresses or shawls and hats or bonnets. It is too light in construction to be a hall hat and coat rack.

LACE BOXES—When fine lace was worn at wrist and throat, fine boxes in which to lock it were in bedchambers of the fashionable, who competed in obtaining boxes of artistic merit.

Although varying considerably in size, the proportions of lace boxes seem to have been fairly constant. Early seventeenth-century specimens are of carved oak, late seventeenth and early eighteenth century, veneered in walnut and other woods or inlaid with "oystershell" veneers or marquetry, *en suite* with the chests on which they stood. Lack of space forbids including more than one example, the beautiful William and Mary box (central, 93). It is covered with figured mulberry veneer and inlaid with the seaweed marquetry fashionable about 1690–1700. It measures $12\frac{3}{4}$ in. by 10 in.

JEWEL CASKETS AND DRESSING CASES—Jewel caskets and fitted dressing cases have played an historic part in women's toilet through the ages. Many, particularly eighteenth-century specimens, are magnificent cabinets, worthy of the jewels they once encased. Pictures of two specimens, chosen for their dissimilarity, are in PLATE 94 and PLATE 95. Caskets of wood, with truncated pyramidal tops and overlays of bone or ivory, bordered with "certosina" marquetry, were made in many parts of Europe, particularly Italy, throughout the Middle Ages. They are extremely difficult to date because so often they are composite, consisting of plaques of various dates and at times different countries, remounted in caskets of later construction. The example illustrated appears to be mainly fifteenth century and the bone carvings bear traces of red paint and gilding. The plaque on the right front has been cut down and obviously was not originally in this casket.

The "rustic" carved casket (centre, 95), with its side hinged trays and watch stand, has been in one family for the last century.

WATCH STANDS—It can be argued with good reason that not all watch stands were bedroom pieces, but whether of definite bedroom type or not, they have been grouped in this section for convenience.

The undoubted bedchamber types, to hold the watch at night, are represented by the three right of PLATE 94 and the double stand (central, 95). This latter, holding a watch and a pocket barometer, is of oak, carved with rope borders enclosing pierced leaf scrolls and flowers and containing a trinket tray at the base, accessible from the open back; it dates from about 1870. The two open pillared stands (right, 94) show the decline of taste about 1840, when the machine had not yet evolved its own suitable design and man tried by speedy mechanical means, to continue making the graceful classical eighteenth-century

96 Elaborately carved boxwood Jester's bauble, Italian, about 1500 A.D.

97 Walnut draughtboard inlaid with engraved ivory and mother of pearl. Dated 1613

98 The cap collecting stick and Georgian spur stand (top row) are rare.
Below, various dog and decoy whistles, bird scarers, toys, etc.

99 Indoor games. *Top right*, an unusual playing card press of the 17th century

forms. Both stands are based on "well head" designs, but their finish is poor, the pillars incorrectly proportioned and the arches consist of unfinished cut-through "turned" circles. One stand is ebonised, the other mahogany, with a mirror inserted in the floor, which unlike a stand of fifty years earlier, no longer has a parquet floor, but is "lined" with black paint to represent stone paving.

The folding watch stand of walnut (foreground) dates from about 1890–1900 and is arranged so that when open it displays the watch at a suitable angle. The exterior, carved with a spray of flowers, is in the foreground of PLATE 95.

Left of PLATE 94, the crude cottage clock tower in mahogany was probably made about 1850. Next, the architectural case, made from a solid pine block, veneered with satinwood, with applied mouldings, is well constructed but a somewhat heavy design of about 1790. The pediment, dentil cornice, frieze and pillasters are all inlaid with ebony and boxwood and there are inlaid fan lunettes in the corners. This case, 9 in. high and 3 in. deep, is typical of the type which I think was not intended as a bedside receptacle for a watch at night; it would have been too troublesome to insert a watch nightly in a small hole 3 in. deep. I think it more likely that cases of this type were deliberately made important for the chimneypiece and intended as permanent receptacles for timepieces which the vagaries of fashion had rendered obsolete for the pocket, but which were too valuable to scrap.

Some watch cases made about this time represented complete façades of buildings. Usually of mahogany, sometimes inlaid in simulation of windows or doors, the circle for the watch commonly appears in a turret or under a pediment at the top of the "building" and in some examples there are drawers in the lower "stories".

Miniature grandfather clocks have been popular from the eighteenth century onwards. The 13¼ in. high mahogany example has an enamelled dial with a sea and landscape scene, in which a miniature windmill has its sails driven by the mechanism. Next, the carved walnut case with "broken" pediment is a fine specimen, dated 1790 and reminiscent in miniature of Liège armoires of that period. The whole case is carved from a single block. The door, which now has on the inside a hook for suspending the watch, originally had a wooden "pocket" for the watch inside it.

Father Time (extreme left, 95) could be mid-seventeenth-century Italian or mid-eighteenth-century English, under Italian influence. I incline to the latter view; the ivy on the tree stump is a very English touch. He is boldly carved from pearwood and the sculptor has skilfully conveyed the appearance of great age in the gnarled fingers and toes and prominent veins. The slightly bowed poise of the figure leaning on the tree stump, with windswept flow of draperies behind him and one hand pointing out the passing time, is excellent. The figure bears traces of polychrome decoration. The scythe is missing.

The carved and polychrome cases, immediately left and right of the casket in the same picture, are English or French and are good representations of the Louis-Quinze Rococo influence which swept England about 1760, much stimulated by the publication of designs in Chippendale's *The Gentleman and Cabinet Maker's Director* (1754). Father Time (left) with his right hand resting on an hour glass, is painted in dark green and gold. The specimen on the right is of better quality; "Atlas" is in natural colour and the Rococo scrolls and base are coloured in faded greens, browns and reds.

The case on the extreme right, dating from about 1780, is an unusual Louis XVI example and has a rather gross figure of a woman reclining at its base. It has suffered from the attention of a "stripper", who has created monotony by removing the polychrome finish to obtain a pickled effect entirely unsuited to the composition.

*   *   *

COLLECTORS NOTES

An interesting bonnet stand, on horseshoe-shaped base containing four drawers, is in the Victoria and Albert Museum, which also contains fine examples of eighteenth-century powdering stands, early mirror frames and mediæval double combs. Examples of the latter are also in the British Museum.

Bed wagons are to be found in Anne of Cleves House, Lewes, the Haslemere Museum, the Rev. C. J. Sharp's Museum, Shepreth, Worthing Museum and Hall-i'-th'-Wood Folk Museum, Bolton.

In the private collection of Commander F. Hart, R.N. (Retd.), at Chipping Campden, are a wig block, with receptacle for curlers and an unusual double wig stand of the seventeenth century, with a turned oak foot and single stem, supporting a crosspiece, on the ends of which are mounted two "mushrooms", giving the general outline of a two-candle candleabra.

Mr. and Mrs. Parker's private Folk Museum at Tickenhill, Bewdley, contains numerous items of bedchamber treen, including a small convex dressing mirror of 1790–1800.

The double wig stand and the wig powdering flask (93), are in Mr. and Mrs. T. W. Bagshawe's collection.

I know no outstanding collection of bedchamber treen, but individual examples occur in museums throughout the country.

100   16th and 17th century draughts pressed from medal dies

101 An outsize chess set of the late 16th or early 17th century

102 Details of the outsize chessmen, compared with normal-sized pieces

PART TWELVE

AMUSEMENT AND EXERCISE

WOODEN devices, although often too large to be treen, have always provided most of man's amusement and exercise. In every century "The fun of the fair" has signified wood: whether in the heyday of maypoles, Punch and Judy, hobby horses, single-stick contests and bouts with cudgels or, more recently, of ring and dart throwing, weight putting, coconut shies, helter-skelters, swings and roundabouts, it's all wood. Likewise are stalls, caravans and framework and furnishing of the "big top".

The jester who lightened the hours of mediæval king, peer or prelate was incomplete without his treen staff or bauble. Some staffs were works of art, like the elaborate one (96), formerly in Cardinal Yorke's collection. Believed Italian, of about 1500, it measures $27\frac{1}{2}$ in. and is carved with a seated lion on top, supporting a shield surmounted by a prelate's hat. Below are a large head with gaping mouth and several carved projections on the stem, representing figures and faces. The remaining surface is sculptured with events in the life of the Virgin, animals, a bird, foliage and scale pattern.

Children are conservative and for many centuries, in many lands, they have played with wooden toys, dolls, building blocks, spades, hoops, skittles, balls, soldiers, kites with wooden winders and ribs and skipping ropes with wooden handles. Nowadays, pogo-sticks, scooters and cars add to the selection of children's conveyances, which already embraced in miniature every wooden vehicle from prams and engines to cars and toboggans, whilst ranging in quality from scale models to adapted soap boxes.

The more exacting adult is equally conservative in his amusements and he, too, has discovered an ideal wood for every pastime.

OUTDOOR PASTIMES—Bowls, popular since the twelfth century, has always used "woods". Since the seventeenth century, nothing has been found to equal lignum vitæ.

Cricket which, in a simple form, dates back as far, would be unimaginable without willow bat, cork filled ball and ash stumps and bails. The springiness of ash, too, has proved ideal for hockey sticks, whilst tennis enthusiasts since the thirteenth century, when tennis was entirely an indoor game played on wooden courts, have acclaimed it for rackets. Beech has provided most tennis racket presses and formerly was used for the heads of wooden golf clubs, which are now made from persimmon wood; hickory shafts have been used since the seventeenth century. This last is also used for skis.

Hornbeam and lignum vitæ are favoured for skittles, called in olden days "kails" in England and "kyles" in Scotland; this was played in England from the fourteenth century and is supposed to have been introduced from Germany. In a sixteenth-century variant of the game, called "club kails", a stick was thrown to knock down the pins. Though often played now with "club" shaped pins and sometimes with round balls, the earlier game used pins shaped like a dunce's cap or bomb with tail end cut off, and a flattish circular ball or "cheese"; an old specimen, which I use as a door stop, is in PLATE 98.

Croquet, reputed to originate from the Stuart game of Pele Mele, was played in St. James's Park, gave its name to Pall Mall and is all wood, excepting the hoops. Pepys in 1661 reports witnessing the game played by the Duke of York. Until 1860 the mallets had barrel or bottle-shaped heads. The shafts are usually ash, occasionally hickory.

If the smaller implements used in blood sports can be classified as treen, there is an enormous selection, from yew wood bows to firearms. Walnut has always ranked foremost for butts of firearms, but cherry was once popular for pistol butts. On the river, cedar is favoured for the Varsity "eights", mahogany for skiffs and the sides of punts, with yellow pine for the bottoms. Spruce is the oarsman's choice.

The greenheart, mostly from British Guiana, seems designed by nature with all the qualities required in a fishing rod. The eighteenth-century "fisherman's companion" (98) is boxwood, $5\frac{3}{4}$ in. high. Each of the ten winders holds separate lines and hooks; the whole device is cleverly carved from one piece. The four weight boxes, which screw into each other, combined form the centre cylinder and are detached "en bloc" by unscrewing the "key". This neat device was formerly in the Evan-Thomas collection, as was the sixteenth- or seventeenth-century powder flask, inlaid with ivory and silver (98).

Wooden stirrups occur in North-West Europe; an example is in PLATE 127. Various types of men's riding boot "jacks" are fairly common, but the rosewood "jack" for a lady's boot (98), designed as a hinged-opening leg and containing its original steel "lifts" is rare, but not as rare as the Georgian mahogany spur stand (central on the same shelf), provided with slots for five pairs of box spurs. Another great rarity is the carved, long-handled yew wood "cap" collecting box (same shelf), designed for easy use at horse level at the hunt. Some old carriage whips have carved decorated handles; their stocks are generally apple, pear or yew. Solid turned wheels or discs, about 5 in. in diameter, ornamentally turned on one face and with 1 to 3 grooves in the rim, are often obtainable. They have a hole through the "hub" for screwing them on the wall; they were used as whip holders; mostly they are mahogany, eighteenth or nineteenth century.

Whistles have provided plenty of fun for wood carvers. That representing a pug dog head (98) has a note irresistible to dogs. The two larger whistles nearby are decoys and give marvellous imitations of different birds. The three-piece clapper alongside is a bird scarer.

Lark catching, a pastime as vicious as bear baiting or cock fighting and likewise now happily obsolete in this country, had its own peculiar treen. This was a snare consisting of a roughly crescent-shaped crossbar, inlaid with pieces of mirror, which was erected on a stake and revolved on a spindle to which a cord was attached. When the cord was jerked, the mirror mounted crossbar rotated rapidly and attracted the larks to the "sportman's" gun.

INDOOR SPORTS—The maple-floored gymnasium with vaulting horse, rowing machine, parallel bars, ladders, poles and old time exercise chair, termed a dandy horse, provides much wood interest but little treen apart from clubs and dumbells, which have changed negligibly through the years.

INDOOR GAMES—The numerous variants of card games are many centuries old. Chess and draughts go back thousands of years. Both are depicted in Egyptian tomb paintings, but probably they originated further East, in India.

The $2\frac{1}{4}$ in. diameter boxwood and ebony, sixteenth- or seventeenth-century European draughts (100), were pressed from medal dies, each commemorating a different event. They are mainly German and most bear dates between 1590 and 1700 and inscriptions in German, Latin or French. Antique draughts were often turned and pressed or carved from a single piece, but all illustrated consist of two separate plaques held apart by a tongue, turned out of the solid wooden rim. The elaborate walnut draughts board (97) is inlaid with engraved ivory and mother-of-pearl, the date 1613 and the name "Jean Ormont of Rouen". The draughts are finely carved, each with different heads.

The Normans are reputed to have introduced chess to the British Isles. Though certainly not fine art, the chessmen and chessboard (101 and 102) are most interesting and their bold but simple turning is very satisfying. Their scale is such that they might have served the inhabitants of Brobdingnag. They are late sixteenth or early seventeenth century, English, and were probably used in some "great hall", where they would have looked appropriate. The size of the "men" has to be seen to be believed. In an endeavour to convey it, I placed "men" from a fairly large ivory set in front of their wooden counterparts, but whilst I was not looking the knight and the bishop changed places! Their heights are as follows·

Kings	12 inches.
Queens	$10\frac{1}{4}$ inches.
Bishops	$9\frac{1}{4}$ inches.
Castles	9 inches.
Knights . . .	8 inches.
Pawns	$7\frac{1}{2}$ inches.

The set is complete and remarkably well preserved. It has suffered from worm at some time and some pieces have split as the result of unequal shrinkage, but substantially it is as made over 300 years ago. All the "white" and most of the "black" men are beech, but some of the latter are ash. Time has faded the "blacks" and darkened the "whites" until now it is difficult to distinguish between them.

The table is most interesting, but somewhat a mystery. It measures 3 ft. 5 in. square, with each of its squares $4\frac{1}{2}$ in. The board is pine and the underframing oak. There is no doubt of the age of either, but they did not start life together, although the board is screwed to the framing by old, hand-made screws. In fact, I feel certain that the underframing was cut down to support the top, which was originally a loose board. That does not solve the whole mystery, however, for the underside of the board is inlaid with two squares of inlaid banding, typical of borders of "Nonesuch" chests made between 1580 and 1640. Does it denote that someone of that period had an inlaid board and found it convenient to make a chessboard on the reverse (for the chess squares are applied and are about $\frac{5}{16}$ in. thick) or was it made originally as a reversible board and ornamental table top? It is also possible that the inlaid frames are not solely ornaments, but were used in some now forgotten game.

For contrast, look at PLATE 103. This magnificent chess set and board, formerly the property of Franz Joseph of Austria, was auctioned in London after the first world war. Of boxwood and ebony, it was commissioned by the Emperor and carved by Ferdinand Juvina of Vienna in 1872. The figures are superb; the white pieces represent Maximilian I with his Consort and entourage, in costume of the period.

The exact date of the invention of playing cards is unknown. They probably originated in India and were in general use in China by 1120. They were known in Europe and recorded in 1262 and are believed to have reached England from France or Italy in the fourteenth century. In early times they were valuable, being hand painted and because very limp they had to be preserved carefully in card presses when not in use. A rare seventeenth-century playing card press is in PLATE 99, together with a well-designed and executed chip carved greywood (dyed sycamore) eighteenth-century card-case and a Regency satinwood card box, fitted for Ecarté, with convex lid studded in marquisite lettering; this gambling game, popular in Regency England, was played in France as early as 1527.

Other useful adjuncts to gambling appear in the same picture. These include two eighteenth-century turretted boxwood dice cups, two concave turned lignum vitæ examples and two inlaid markers containing compartments for pegs. The masur burr birch box and counter trays are all turned from the same block. The "Pope Joan" board, with its radiating divisions, is lacquered green and gold. Above are a selection of eighteenth-century inlaid cribbage boards; cribbage, believed to be of English origin, goes back at least to 1674.

The rosewood cup and ball game (centre, 98), known as bilboquet, was popular in Georgian days and one is depicted in a picture entitled "Blind Man's Buff", painted by Sir David Wilkie in 1813 for the Prince Regent; it now hangs in Buckingham Palace. Some of the eighteenth-century spinning tops, also in PLATE 98, are hollow and, when spun, make a most engaging noise, due to the lead shot which they contain. The two Welsh costume tumbler toys on their rosy apple bases (extreme right) are late eighteenth or early nineteenth century. In spite of their costume, they were probably made in England.

The method formerly used in Germany for making simple wooden toys was most ingenious. In Saxony a circular ring was lathe-turned, so that its section formed the outline of the desired animal. The ring was then sliced radially, the cut-through sections forming rough models of the animals. A number of rings and the animals or other objects formed from them are shown in various stages in PLATE 104. This method saves much labour, but some deft movements with a hand carving chisel and a paint brush are still needed to convert the sawn sections into completed articles.

Until the end of the eighteenth century, when organised toy making began and much output was trash, wood provided 99 per cent. of youth's amusements. Most pieces which have survived, including dolls' houses, their furniture, as well as their china, glass, silver, etc., are miniature editions of full-sized pieces. These pieces were actually made by cabinetmakers, including some of the most famous, and by turners, china modellers, glass blowers and silversmiths. A few examples are in PLATE 105. The tiny painted tea set on tray is all painted wood. The table on which it sits is veneered in burr walnut. On the circular mahogany table, the miniature boxwood snuff boxes are complete with tortoiseshell linings and one of the cups is Tunbridge "stick ware". Some interesting model chairs are included, as well as a chest of drawers, a spinning wheel and an Italian eighteenth-century jointed wooden puppet.

The little lady under the glass shade, standing on the beautifully made mahogany tripod torchère, proves that there is nothing new under the sun. With all her goods and chattels on her head and back, she is obviously the ancestor of our own unhappy squatters.

*　　　*　　　*

COLLECTORS NOTES

Many of our museums contain treen of the type illustrated.

Amongst adult indoor amusements not included in these illustrations, there are, in various galleries, numerous examples of halma, ludo, snakes and ladders, some with painted wood boards, also "Fox and Geese" and "Solitaire" boards. Bishop Hooper's Lodgings Folk Museum, Gloucester, has a solitaire board in which wooden pegs substitute glass marbles. Luton Museum and the Pitt Rivers Museum, Oxford, contain comprehensive collections of toys and games. The British Museum has fine Egyptian chess and draughts boards, as well as specimens of pressed commemoration medal draughts, like those illustrated.

The Victoria and Albert Museum possesses fine specimens of games boards, including an exceptionally handsome Dutch walnut draughts and backgammon board of about 1660. The draughts are carved with animals on both sides. The jester's staff illustrated is also in this museum.

An outstandingly beautiful sixteenth-century, carved walnut wood whistle in the Wallace Collection bears the carved and gilded cypher and monogram of Diane de Poitiers, mistress of

103   A magnificent chess set made for the late Franz Joseph of Austria by Ferdinand Juvina of Vienna

104   Ring cut Saxony toys

Henri II. Also in the Wallace Collection are carved draughts and a fine eighteenth-century French wood engraving block, cut to print twenty court cards in duplicate.

Toys of bygone days are displayed in London at the Bethnal Green and Geffrye Museums and at Kensington Palace. The National Museum of Wales, Cardiff, has, among other interesting items, some wooden clappers formerly used by children in certain parts of Wales at Eastertime in collecting Easter eggs. During the week before Easter children used to visit farmhouses and shops in their parishes to beg for eggs.

Examples of "baby cages", known in the eighteenth century alternatively as toddlers' go-carts, baby cages, baby trotters or walking cradles, are in Luton Museum, the Rev. C. J. Sharp's Museum, Shepreth, the Cambridge and County Folk Museum and the Victoria and Albert Museum. The latter has an interesting mid seventeenth-century carved wood rocking horse, with contemporary trappings; also numerous period dolls' houses.

Mr. and Mrs. J. F. Parker's private Folk Museum at Tickenhill, Bewdley, contains a grand nursery section with dolls, toys and games of past ages to delight the hearts of children of all ages. Among particularly interesting examples are an eighteenth-century singing "diabolo" made of pearwood, a pair of adjustable stilts of about 1800 and a seventeenth-century baby cage.

In Museum No. 3 of the Royal Botanic Gardens, Kew, is the Saxony "toy ring" (104). Lark snares or bird catcher's mirrors are to be found in the museum at Devizes, the Rev. C. J. Sharp's Museum, Shepreth, and at Worthing Museum.

Hove Museum has a curious eighteenth-century table game, called "Toad in the Hole", which seems to be the forerunner of modern pin-tables.

Turned whip holders are in many museums, including Cheltenham, Bishop Hooper's Lodgings, Gloucester, and Tickenhill Manor.

PART THIRTEEN

THE TRAVELLER'S DEBT TO WOOD

TRAVEL'S vicissitudes have been many, but its debt to wood continuous. Neolithic man, 5,000 years ago, made sledges from conveniently forked branches, lashed with cross branches, and canoes from alternately burned and chipped-out logs. At least 4,000 years ago Asiatics used pack animals to carry wooden boxes of merchandise and personal belongings. Five thousand years ago the Sumerians used carts with solid wooden wheels. The Egyptians, 3,500 years ago, used log rollers for moving heavy stones and 3,350 years ago they had chariots with spoked wheels and leather tyres. It was left to the Romans of over 2,000 years ago to build good roads and bridges, which enabled European wheels to turn on a large scale. In mediæval times these roads fell into disrepair and until the sixteenth century in England travel reverted to horseback again. Stage-wagons appeared in the sixteenth century and, towards its end, began to offer uncomfortable, unsafe and irregular services between important towns, but speed, with six to eight horses pulling, only averaged 4 miles an hour, due to bad road conditions, which caused frequent mishaps.

The Science Museum, South Kensington, contains many original examples of seventeenth to nineteenth century conveyances, as well as show-cases representing travel through the ages.

The mid-seventeenth century produced that improvement on the stage wagon—the wooden stage coach; thereafter, with improving roads, comfort and speed both increased. Initially stage coaches, which were unsprung, only carried inside passengers, but as travellers increased, "outsides" were allowed to hang on, as best they could, to the luggage piled roof. Outside accommodation soon improved and by 1760 the "quality" travelled outside and their servants were relegated to the musty interior. About 1767, a basket, termed the "conveniency", was attached to the back of the coach for half-price passengers. In 1789 the introduction of springing for coaches increased comfort greatly. In 1785 the first mail coach had been introduced and by 1800 lighter vehicles of the flying coach and post chaise type began to run and are said to have accomplished the fifty-two mile journey to Brighton in only eight hours. In 1818 the wooden hobbyhorse, ancestor of the modern bicycle, appeared and attained a speed of ten miles per hour on the level.

TREEN FOR WALKING—Walking, in former days, produced its treen. Wooden sabots were largely used and one of them, hurled into a loom by a French textile worker on strike in 1890, produced the word "sabotage". Wooden pattens were used to protect shoes and feet in bad weather until well into the nineteenth century, but it was Hitler in the nineteen forties who brought us back to wooden-soled shoes.

Men who did not carry swords, took staffs or cudgels. Women used more elegant sticks and the stick was as essential to the blind as the wooden crutch or peg-leg to the maimed.

The pedlar had his special shaped stick, for carrying across his shoulder, with his pack slung on the end. An ashwood example, 37 in. long, is in PLATE 108. These sticks must have been made in thousands, but are now rare. Stallkeepers and pedlars, until well into the nineteenth century, held a much larger proportion of trade than they have now. Owing to the impossible state of the roads, people in country districts largely depended on pedlars on foot and with pack horses for many necessities and nearly all

105 Selection of miniature furniture

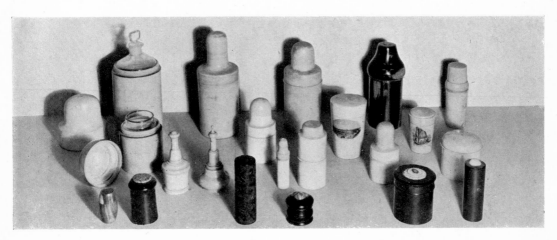

106 Travelling bottle and tumbler cases, glove powdering flasks and powder pots

107 Travelling candle holders, cased mirrors, pipe case, *etuis* and ink bottle

109   Oak campaigning chest with original Liége bottles of *circa* 1780

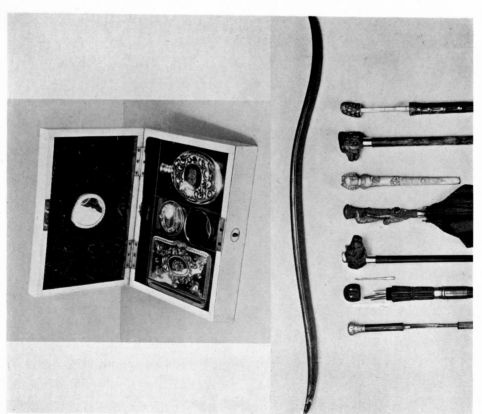

108   A 19th century luncheon box with original fittings. A pedlar's pack stick and a selection of quaintly carved parasol handles and "fitted" sticks

luxuries. Sixteenth-century town cries show that pedlars between them carried a range worthy of a departmental store.

Delightful oddities, as also very beautiful wood carvings, have been incorporated in stick and umbrella handles. A few are in PLATE 108. The second from the left contains, in the handle a serviceable kit of woodworkers tools. The handle unscrews and contains a "chuck", in which the desired tool can be mounted. The elegant ebony stick (third left) has for handle an intelligent looking carved bull, with in-curling horns. The sixth, a Georgian mahogany "two-face", is carved on one side to represent a snarling boar, whilst in reverse is a judge. The bamboo stick (right) contains a rule, divided into "hands", for measuring horses.

Good quality walking sticks, dating from earlier than about 1775–80, usually belonged to women, old people or young fops; the latter delighted themselves and annoyed others by carrying long canes with clouded amber heads, which they hung on a blue ribbon from the third button of their coats. The feeling of the time towards them is conveyed in the stickman's "cry":

> *"I've sticks and canes for old and young*
> *To either they are handy,*
> *In driving off a barking cur,*
> *Or chastising a dandy."*

Normally, men of fashion who used swords, carried them until about 1775 and when they changed to canes, these often contained swords, as in PLATE 108, left.

Umbrellas, as state canopies and for protection against sun and rain, date from early days and were known to the ancient Assyrians, Persians and Egyptians. The Chinese used umbrellas in the eleventh century. The Maratha princes were also "Lords of the Umbrella" and the twelfth-century Doges of Venice had state umbrellas. These umbrellas, pictures of which survive, were mostly permanent canopies, although some appear to have taken apart. Some form of umbrella was known in Anglo Saxon England, but we do not know its construction. An inventory made for Mary Queen of Scots in 1561, described a satin covered umbrella with a golden fringe.

The first man credited with carrying a modern folding umbrella in London was Jonas Hanway, the traveller and philanthropist, whose fulminations against tea drinking aroused the ire of Dr. Johnson. Hanway, reported to have carried his umbrella first in 1778, was jeered by the London mob because, since the introduction of the modern form into England about 1700, umbrellas had only been carried by women. Caustic comment on a young man who used an umbrella in 1709 was recorded in an advertisement in the December issue of the *Female Tatler*:

> "The young gentleman, that for fear of the rain, borrowed the umbrella at Will's coffee house in Cornhill, . . . is hereby advertised that to be dry from head to foot on the like occasion, he shall be welcome to the maid's pattens."

Another reason, undoubtedly, why Englishmen of that time regarded umbrellas as effeminate was because they had come from France. In Scotland, an Edinburgh surgeon in 1780 and in Glasgow another surgeon in 1781 are credited with the introduction. In 1787, Parson Woodforde's diary records that at a funeral he succumbed to having an umbrella held over his head during a blizzard.

The centre handle in the row in PLATE 108 is an amusing Victorian example, carved as a rough tree, out of which a gnome near the top is leaning and lending a helping hand to another gnome, who has become wedged in a hole lower down. Right of this example is a nineteenth-century beautifully carved boxwood handle, in the form of a girl's head; it is probably French.

TREEN FOR TRAVELLING—In the nineteenth century, travel, though vastly speeded and improved by the railways, still necessitated much more baggage than is needed to-day, due to discomfort on the journey, unsuitable packaging of toilet necessities, small likelihood of being able to purchase many requirements at the journey's end and the probable low standard of accommodation available. Until the end of the century, if staying away more than a few days, it was quite usual to take a hip bath and a heavy wooden trunk filled with a large selection of turned wood boxes, to hold the various articles needed for comfort.

In PLATE 106 is a good selection of wooden bottle cases and other articles of like nature, carried around by our grandparents. All the bottle cases illustrated are boxwood, except one (back row), which is lignum vitæ. All are as sound and serviceable to-day as when first made. That at the left end of the second row contains a jar, sealed by a cork pad inserted in the screw-on lid. The two cases embellished with views (right end, same row) hold tumblers.

The glove powdering flasks, near the left, differ from those in PLATE 92 by having screw-on caps. In front are a selection of screw-topped powder pots and boxes, mostly ebony. The cylindrical ebony box, carved in low relief with shamrocks, is one of those usually sold to credulous travellers in Ireland as "Irish bog oak". The small barrel-shaped, lignum vitæ box (left) contains a smelling salts bottle. Further travelling treen is in PLATE 107. In the back row (left) are three nineteenth-century travelling candle-sticks, the interiors of which are shown in PLATE 120. The architectural boxwood pillar on the left contains a candle and the base a roomy box for matches. There is a striker underneath; the urn on top of the pillar holds the "good-night" match. The walnut wood double bowl next, opens out into two chamber candlesticks, the sockets of which unscrew and store in the bowls. The domed boxwood pillar is ingenious and unusual. The pillar, which is the candlecover, unscrews and the threaded nipple on its summit screws into the aperature in the base and becomes a handle, as PLATE 120 shows. The small knob at the side of the base forms a cover for the match receptacle and there is a striker underneath. The sycamore double bowl (right), usually described as a travel-ling butter dish, is really a traveller's butter dish, in which samples of butter were taken to market. Double bowls, similar in form but lighter, are sometimes found. They are invariably characterised by a peculiar musty odour and were used as travelling soap boxes in the eighteenth century.

Extreme right are two travelling mirror cases, with sliding shutters to protect the precious glass; both are chip carved in geometrical patterns. That in the background is mahogany and, therefore, almost certainly eighteenth century, which is late for this form of case. The carving in its inlay is crudely filled with red and black sealing wax. The other example is walnut and is typical of the seventeenth century; some of the back-ground is coloured in red and green. Besides the frames is a travelling ink bottle and, behind, an eighteenth-century Dutch boxwood pocket case for a clay pipe, of which other examples are in PLATE 58.

Many other objects described in different parts of this book are really travelling treen in this sense, such as some snuff and tobacco boxes illustrated in Part 6, the folding book rest (63), and the travelling bookcase (62).

The other objects in PLATE 107 are part of great-grandmother's sewing and mend-ing kit. These include two nineteenth-century "pears", which combine darning eggs with receptacles for needles, thread and thimbles; the inverted cone in the background, another variant of the same device, has three separate receptacles for the same articles; two eighteenth-century *étius* appear in the foreground.

On the journey, during most of the nineteenth century, the traveller carried his refreshments and some of the fitted luncheon boxes made about 1870–80 are most attractive. The example in PLATE 108 is of oak, overlaid externally with ivory and lined with blue velvet. All its fittings are original, including an ivory framed mirror, an engraved silver sandwich box and brandy flask, a silver-mounted horn beaker, a silver topped finger bowl and even the original serviette with drawn thread fringe, which lies under the lid in the back compartment. It was made for the Rev. William Cashel Stewart (1844–1902), Vicar of South Cave, Yorkshire. He was the fourth son of Robert, second Earl of Castle Stewart, and the box has his coat of arms in ivory on the lid and engraved on the silver fittings.

Campaigning in the late eighteenth century seems to have had its points, at any rate for higher ranks. The oak campaigning chest (109), measuring $22\frac{1}{2}$ in. by $11\frac{1}{2}$ in. by $12\frac{1}{2}$ in. high, contains its fourteen original Liège glass liquor bottles of about 1780.

Talking of bottles brings us to apothecaries' travelling cases and household portable medicine chests. These were most ingenious and, in the eighteenth century especially, were fine examples of cabinetmaking. I have examples dating from the seventeenth to the late nineteenth century. Several of them have secret drawers for poisons. Lack of space precludes illustration and these will be described and illustrated in another book.

*　　　*　　　*

COLLECTORS NOTES

Finely fitted travelling cases are in the Wallace Collection and the Victoria and Albert Museum. The latter, as well as the London Museum and the Bethnal Green Museum, also include sticks, umbrellas and parasols among their fine costume collections. Luton Public Museum has an interesting eighteenth-century travelling shaving set in mahogany case.

A magnificent and well worn travelling canteen and dressing case, used by the First Duke of Wellington during most of his life, was shown by the present Duke at the Regency Exhibition, Brighton (1946).

Hove Museum displays a fine eighteenth-century mahogany folding wig stand. It consists of two thin fret cut strips, which interlock together at right angles, like a modern millinery stand; it is illustrated in *Dictionary of Furniture* by Percy Macquoid.

Strong boxes, specially designed for travel by coach, were made in the seventeenth and eighteenth centuries. They were constructed of heavy timber, steel banded and with hinged lids and intricate locks. Their carcase ends were made sufficiently stout to contain in their thickness square headed bolts, which passed through the bottom of the box and bolted it to the timber of the coach. The bolt heads were recessed into the top edges of the carcase ends and were turned by detachable square keys, so that when the boxes were once locked, it was impossible to tamper with the bolts.

PART FOURTEEN

MISCELLANEOUS TOOLS AND APPLIANCES

WHEN Churchill said "Give us the tools and we will finish the job", he was expanding Carlyle's earlier utterance: "Man is a tool using animal . . . without tools he is nothing, with tools he is all". Unfortunately, the dividing line is thin between tools for peace and war and the first sticks used by man as defence against animals, soon became spears, clubs and bows and arrows. The hunted became hunters and from hunting animals for food, it was a short step for men to kill their fellows for the same purpose, or to propitiate angry Gods, or for sheer lust of conquest and greed for booty.

Tools of war have no place in this book; we are more concerned with the tools which man has made to raise his standard of living; high amongst these rank the woodworking tools used to make the objects illustrated here.

WOODWORKING TOOLS—A showcase at the Science Museum, South Kensington, illustrating the evolution of hand tools, demonstrates that basically woodworking and many other hand tools have changed little for centuries. Axes, adzes, hammers, mallets, chisels, gouges, saws, spokeshaves, bradawls, braces and bits and pincers have kept the same form. A mason's mallet found in an Egyptian tomb of 1370 B.C. is almost identical with one used to-day. But the range of specialised tools has increased gradually and since the sixteenth century planes have largely superseded adzes, while screws have occasioned screwdrivers. The main differences is that formerly tools were, wherever practicable, made beautiful, often by the hands which used them, whilst now they are strictly utilitarian, mass produced and shop supplied. Nevertheless, functionally they have improved greatly, owing to improvements in steel.

Machinery, apart from its own principle of rotating, has evolved practically no new woodcutting principles. Saw benches are only revolving circular saw blades, whilst planers, spindles and tenoners employ square planing or moulding cutters, bolted on a revolving block. The cutting chain used on a chain saw and that on a morticer are the only really modern woodworking innovations I can recall. Even the router, that miracle tool of the modern factory, is only a "bit" or cutter, revolving in a chuck at the incredible speed of 20,000–30,000 revolutions a minute.

The four planes (110) exemplify the work which old time craftsmen put into their tools. The early eighteenth-century, long beechwood plane (in background) measures $26\frac{1}{2}$ in. In addition to the carving on the handle, the front forms a grotesque face, composed of leaf scrolls. A certain type of modern routing plane, with narrow iron, is familiarly known to woodworkers as an "old woman's tooth", but I doubt whether many who use it know that formerly it was apparently made in the form of a grotesque face, the shavings being ejected from the old woman's mouth. Whether shape created name, or name inspired design, I know not, but the amusing walnut example (centre) provides one of my most interesting and treasured "finds". It appears to be seventeenth century, probably of French origin. The beechwood adjustable fillister plane (left) is a fine and much used specimen, carved with the date 1764. Its fence is moulded from the solid and contains most efficient wedge stops. The skew-mouthed side-moulding plane (right), also of beech, is dated 1729.

In PLATE 111 is a further selection of old English tools. The hammer, signed "Leander Green 1694", is $12\frac{1}{4}$ in. long; the beechwood jointer plane, with carved handles, dated 1771, is 31 in. long. The moulding plane, stamped "Michael Saxby & F.C., 1756",

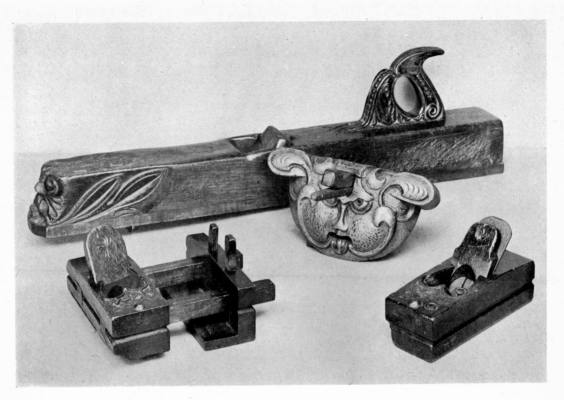

110   17th and 18th century carved planes

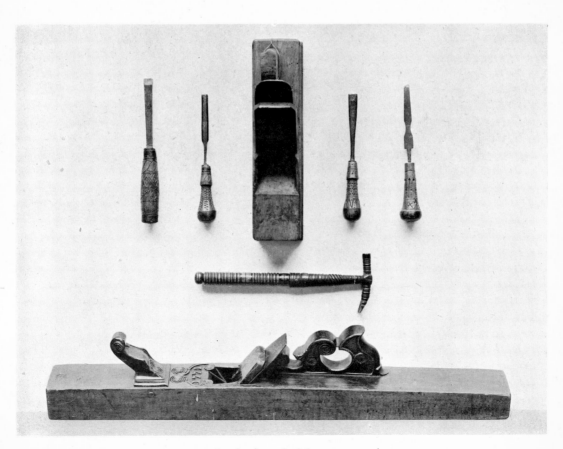

111   A selection of 18th century tools

112   Carved bookbinder's stretcher, French, 17th century

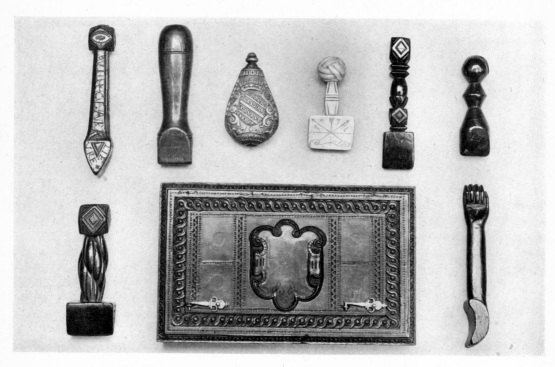

113   Sailmakers' tools, fine quality boxwood chrism bottle of 1725, and the 17th century box for scales illustrated in 68

114   Miscellaneous tools and appliances

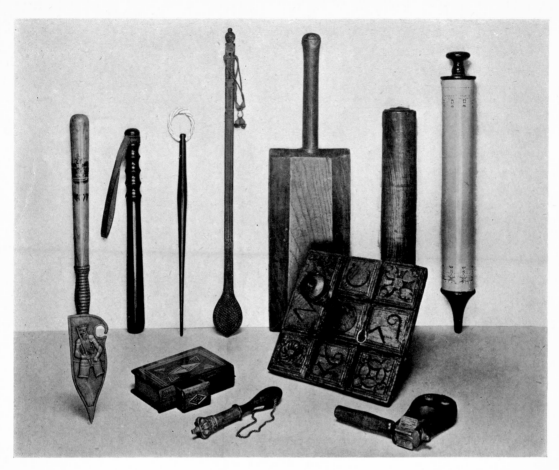

115 Button cleaning stick, constables' staffs, back scratchers, mangling board and roller, dust bellows, home safe, tipstaff, hat peg of 1679 and "rattle"

116 Oyster opener

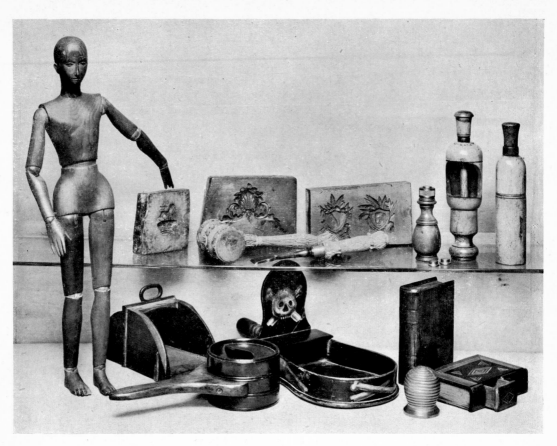

117   Compo moulds, bottle corking and stamping devices.   Artist's lay figure.   Collecting
and money boxes

118   Printing set, top hat and glove blocks, braidmaker's hand loom, goffering stack
and waist measuring rule

front of the pocket-size stick, has a separate "ramrod". It has been suggested that it was for loading a muzzle-loader. The small rosewood tube in front (extreme left) contains a spring loaded needle, the point of which emerges about $\frac{3}{16}$ in. when the knob at the other end is pressed. Possibly it was used as a scarifying needle.

The purpose of the beechwood tongs (right) is unknown, but they appear to possess considerable antiquity and show signs of wear. The small implement in front of them, with two hook-ended pivoted arms, is made to fold and the two arms are held closed by the screw cap seen at the side. It is apparently some kind of "race".

Central in PLATE 113 is the beautiful carved walnut case of about 1650, which contains the diamond merchant's scales, illustrated open in PLATE 68 and described in Part 8. Immediately above is an extremely finely carved Italian chrism bottle of boxwood. On one side is a coronet above a coat of arms and the date 1725; on the reverse a Monstrance in a foliated border.

The curious backboard (115) divided into nine carved elm panels, with a long walnut peg piercing the centre lozenge and continuing through for inserting into a wall, is the parson's hat peg from Loxton Church, Somerset. Dated 1679, in which year there was a change of incumbent, the carved initials "N.C." fit neither the old nor new parson, so they probably refer to the carver or donor.

The artist's or sculptor's layfigure (117) is pine, carefully and tightly ball-jointed so that it can be arranged in any position. Nearby are a well-carved boxwood ceremonial mallet and chisel and three boxwood moulds for compo ornament. Compo, consisting of glue, linseed oil and whitening, was used largely in the eighteenth century to apply ornament to chimney pieces, panelling and other interior woodworks and the range of ornament to be found in reverse in the blocks, covers some of the finest examples of Adam and contemporary French work. Moulds for plasterwork may be found dating from considerably earlier. The carving of all these blocks was a specialised art, calling for unusual skill. The best of the small and fine examples are generally made of boxwood, on account of its unusual hardness and close grain and the long wear it gives, as well as the fine polished surface which it imparts to the "compo". The moulds were carved in reverse, direct from a drawing.

Second left (118) is a top-hat maker's mould or block and next is a glove-maker's sectional stretching block, both nineteenth century and adjustable in size by insertion or removal of separate sections. One from the right, the late eighteenth or early nineteenth-century device, is a braidmaker's hand loom, of a type believed to have been introduced from Scandinavia. In the same picture is a quaint eighteenth or nineteenth-century waist measurer.

*　　　*　　　*

COLLECTORS NOTES

The Geffrye Museum, Kingsland Road, the Haslemere Museum and the Victoria and Albert Museum all have good collections of old time woodworkers' tools. The last named also possesses the bookbinder's stretcher illustrated. Hove Museum has an outsize jointer plane. It is English, 33 ins. long, of elaborately carved walnut, dated 1672.

The British, London and Guildhall Museums all contain collections of mediæval tools and appliances excavated in London. Though by reason of age, the wooden parts have usually disappeared, it is interesting to examine the form of the surviving metal and to see how little many familiar objects have changed during a period of 600 years or more.

The Pitt Rivers Museum, Oxford, specialises in primitive tools and Hull Museum of Commerce and Transport has implements and devices formerly employed in local industries.

The Wallace Collection has a fine sixteenth-century German case for a prayer book. It is pearwood, decorated with pierced Gothic tracery.

In addition to a general collection of trade tools and appliances, Luton Public Museum displays an unrivalled selection of wooden objects appertaining to straw work. Splint mills, plait mills, rolling pins and boards for straw plaits, straw sorters, etc., are fully described in *The Romance of the Straw Hat*, published by Luton Museum. Braintree Town Hall Museum is also well represented with straw plaiting implements.

The National Museum of Wales, Cardiff, is the place to visit for old Welsh industrial tools and devices. It also contains an eighteenth-century gauffering stack, as does the Rev. C. J. Sharp's Museum, Shepreth. The Georgian House Museum, Bristol, has a gauffering board and ribbed roller and an interesting nineteenth-century washing machine, formed like a rocking cradle with a scrubbing board on top and there is also a ponderous mangling table with heavy oak frame, three rollers and a cogged wheel, which drives a weighted box backwards and forwards by winding and unwinding leather straps. It is really a semi-mechanical form of the mangling board and roller described in this chapter. The earliest and finest specimen of this contraption which I have seen is in the private collection of Commander F. Hart, R.N. (Retd.), at Chipping Campden. It is of eighteenth-century panelled oak construction. Box mangles are also in Luton Museum, the Cambridge and County Folk Museum, Hall-i'-th'-Wood Folk Museum, Bolton, and Anne of Cleves House, Lewes. The last named has an unusual kettle or iron holder, consisting of a circular turned rod, split in two, hinged and hollowed to fit a handle.

Hall-i'-th'-Wood Folk Museum has a gauffering stack and Worthing Museum a "slickenstone" made of wood. Slickenstones take the form of large mushrooms, usually of stone or glass, with stumpy stalks as handles and were used for smoothing linen before flat-irons were invented.

Wooden pitch pipes are in numerous museums, including Cheltenham, the Rev. C. J. Sharp's Museum, Shepreth, Anne of Cleves House, Lewes, etc. They were used from 100 to 200 years ago, to give the keynote before singing commenced in church. The pipes have pistons marked with the names of the notes; the piston is withdrawn until the required note is exposed, when the pipe is blown.

The Museum of Fisheries and Shipping, Hull, has a good collection of sail smoothing implements, also several fids. Cheltenham Museum also possesses specimens. The king of all fids, which is of lignum vitae, 52 *in. long and* 11 *in. in diameter at the base*, stands in Worthing Museum, where are also a mangling board and roller, similar to those illustrated.

If you meet a piece of wood about 2 ft. long, $1\frac{3}{4}$ in. at its greatest width and $1\frac{3}{8}$ in. thick, shaped like a bird's outstretched wings, you have found a "gambrel", sometimes called "gambrel-hogh" or "gambrel stick", which is the stick upon which a pig was hung to be scraped or cleaned. The stick was notched so that it could be used for various sized animals. In Suffolk it was used to suspend sheep, hogs and calves. A gambrel carved from ashwood is in Cheltenham Museum, which also possesses an amusing "stocks", used in a dame's school about 1820, for correcting round shoulders. There is also a "fleam mallet holder", used in conjunction with fleams for bleeding horses and a "balling gun" for administering pills to horses.

An oyster measurer is in St. Helier's Museum, Jersey. Colchester Museum, which has the oyster opener illustrated in PLATE 116, has recently acquired a quaint piece—a "deportment stocks". It is a beech board, 21 in. long by 10 in. wide, with a cut-out centre, shaped so that the child who was to be punished or whose deportment was to be improved, could stand in it and curtsy a given number of times, whilst holding that joy of the Georgians and Victorians, a "back-board". Backboards, either "T" shaped or long strips of wood, wide in the centre and curving to narrow ends, were passed behind the back and held in the crook of the arms to straighten the back. The Cambridge and County Folk Museum, the Hertfordshire County Museum, St. Albans, Cheltenham Museum and Brighton Museum all have specimens.

Interesting and unusual pieces, including wooden drop weight rodent traps of the type in PLATE 38, are in several museums including the Rev. C. J. Sharp's, the Geffrye Museum, the Stranger's Hall Museum, Norwich, Worthing Museum, Barbican House Museum, Lewes, and Mr. and Mrs. J. F. Parker's private Folk Museum at Tickenhill, Bewdley. The latter has many items of interest appertaining to this chapter, including a box mangle, a rocking cradle washing machine, lace washing tongs for handling delicate lace, gambrels and a hair-curler press.

Wood engraving blocks are in various museums. The Hancock Museum, Newcastle-on-Tyne, has a collection of Thomas Bewick's original drawings and woodcuts. In addition to blocks for printing and illustrating packs of cards and books, interesting and decorative specimens to collect are those designed for printing patterned textiles and wallpapers. The place to study the last named is not a museum but a farmyard near Henley-on-Thames, which has a barn, the gable end of which presents a unique surface texture, being entirely formed from wood blocks in rich floral designs, scrolls and formal patterns.

PART FIFTEEN

BY FIRE AND CANDLE LIGHT
FIRE MAKING

ARTIFICIAL light, heat and power are three of wood's greatest contributions to civilisation. The ability to make fire was probably the first step in man's ascent and ascendency over beast. Some uses of fire in the recent war were a pathetic symbol of the re-ascendancy of the beast in man.

The first lights to shine from cavemen's homes and the illuminants for the execution of their mural paintings and engravings came from wood plucked from the fire. For countless centuries raw wood fed these fires, which served for heating, cooking and scaring wild beasts and played an important part in tribal magic and religious ceremonies.

Originally, doubtless, man obtained some basic flames from natural sources, such as volcanoes, lightning-struck trees and sun-caused conflagrations, but such spasmodic and inconvenient sources and the impossibility of replacing an extinguished fire undoubtedly originated the sacred and eternal fires of the temples.

THE SPARK—Although early man solved the problem of fire making at will, all the methods employed were tedious. Fire making developed on four different lines:

(1) A controlled version of nature's sun-caused conflagrations by introduction of a burning glass.
(2) Striking a flint with a nodule of iron pyrites.
(3) Wood friction methods.
(4) The fire piston.

The first never developed into any modern invention, but the second, when man learnt to smelt iron, became flint and steel used in conjunction with tinder boxes which, in their most advanced forms, became tinder pistols and eventually tinder lighters; the latter, by refinement and changing their tinder for wicks and petrol, have become petrol lighters. The third was improved by coating the striking surfaces of the wood with chemical compounds, thus forming friction matches, whilst the fourth, invented quite early by primitive people and confined to South-East Asia and the East Indies, consisted of a small cylinder, closed at one end, in which was placed a minute piece of tinder and a tight-fitting removable piston; the piston, on being placed in the cylinder, was struck a sharp blow and immediately withdrawn, when the air compression and engendered heat had ignited the tinder. Fire pistons were usually made of horn or wood; a wooden specimen is in front of PLATE 119. The principle was rediscovered and patented in Britain in 1807, when fire pistols or syringes were made of steel and brass.

The inconveniences of tinder boxes were manifest: damp defeated, strong draughts delayed them. They often had to be operated in darkness and whilst a light was obtained occasionally in less than three minutes, it sometimes took up to half an hour, under unfavourable conditions. It is not, therefore, surprising that it was common to keep a fire burning all the year round until friction matches became general. There were much earlier so-called matches, but they did not strike: they were sulphur-tipped strips of wood, cardboard, paper, woven cotton or straw—merely adjuncts of the tinder box and actually secondary tinder for conveying flame from the smouldering basic tinder to candle, rushlight or smoker's pipe. The usual tinder in domestic tinder boxes was charred linen rags, but dry grass, powdered leaves, rotten wood, down from birds and "amadou" were all used. Amadou, or German tinder, is a fungus which grows on dead trees and when prepared looks like brown washleather.

INSTANTANEOUS LIGHT CONTRIVANCES—The numerous devices which intervened between tinder and flint methods and friction matches, were known collectively as "Instantaneous Light Contrivances". Among the earliest was the "Phosphorus Box", invented in Italy in 1786. It contained a bottle of phosphorus and sulphur tipped matches which, when dipped in the bottle, ignited. An improved version, introduced into England from France about 1810, had the bottle filled with sulphuric acid and the matches tipped with a hard paste, composed of potassium chlorate, sugar and gum. The majority of English boxes are tin; treen are rare, but a few wooden examples, mostly stamped "Berry's Patent", survive. Three are in PLATE 119; they are the first three on the left in front. The simple turned lignum cylinder, with projecting base and screw-on tapering dome lid at side, is English, period 1810–25. The bottle of acid, which is missing, fitted in the inner ring, with the matches surrounding it in a separate ring. The lid contains a projecting inner ring, which clamps tightly on the bottle of acid. Next is a plain rosewood cylinder, a French patent of approximately the same period, in which the lid is secured by "hit and miss" projections. The projecting neck of the glass bottle shows in the photograph. It is spring seated, so that the top of the bottle is always forced tightly against the inner ring in the lid. The outer ring of the box contains three separate compartments for small candles, one for matches and two others of unknown purpose. The more elaborate turned ebony box, with funnel-shaped top, is one of Berry's patents of about 1825–35, which has a separate lid for the acid bottle, so that matches stored in the outer ring remained protected while a single match was dipped in the bottle.

MATCHES—The need for tinder boxes and Instantaneous Light Contrivances died soon after 1826, when John Walker, a Stockton-on-Tees chemist, invented and sold his first "friction" lights at 1s. per box of 50, including a piece of sandpaper, between the folds of which the match head was inserted sharply, causing it to ignite—provided the head remained attached. Initially the invention achieved little popularity and Walker only sold 250 boxes in the first 2½ years. Little over a century later, no fewer than 8,640,000,000 were sold in Great Britain within a similar period. Walker, indentured to become a doctor, abandoned medicine for chemistry and during his firemaking experiments a stick, which had been dipped in a composition of potassium chlorate and antimony sulphide, ignited when rubbed accidentally and gave birth to his invention. Walker's matches contained no phosphorus.

PROTECTIVE MATCH BOXES—Phosphorus matches were introduced to England by German and Austrian chemists about 1830 and their greater ease in striking gained them quick popularity. Their liability to spontaneous combustion from a knock or through exposure to warmth was so great, however, that it strictly limited them to home use and urgently necessitated provision of special containers, known as "Protective Match Boxes". These, like "Instantaneous Light Contrivances", were mostly metal. Treen specimens are rare. Tinned iron were commonest, but brass, copper, white metal, marble, bone and ivory were all made. One of the latter is shown among the treen, a comprehensive selection of which are illustrated with the "Instantaneous Light Contrivances" (119). They are invariably well made, usually from lignum vitæ or ebony. Some, like four on the left, back row, are combined with candleholders and all except one have sinkings under their bases for circular "strikers" of glasspaper. The exception, the third candleholder from the left, is battlemented and has circular engraved rings to simulate stonework. These rings act as strikers.

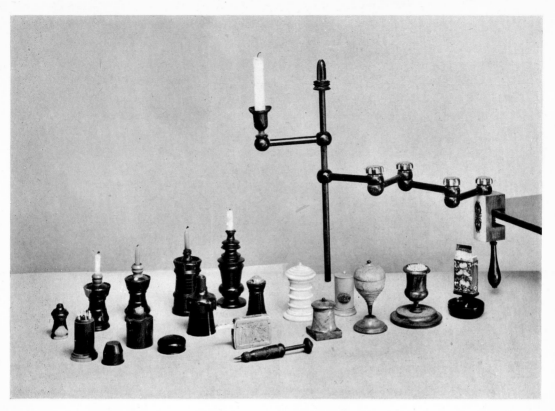

119   Instantaneous light contrivances, protective match boxes, and a Tunbridge ware candle arm

120   Spill vases, and candle holders for travelling

121　Elaborately carved Italian Renaissance bellows

122　Italian carved pricket candlesticks of the 16th and 17th century and
domestic candle holders of the 18th century

When phosphorus matches superseded Berry's "Instantaneous Light Contrivances", he converted some of the latter into protective boxes by fitting circular strikers into the centre compartments, formerly housing the bottles of sulphuric acid; consequently "Instantaneous Light Contrivances" and "Protective Match Boxes" are sometimes found with similar exteriors. Most protective boxes have a small brass or bone boss inserted either at the summit or near the edge of the top, for holding a single match. This was used while getting in or out of bed, after extinguishing or before lighting the gas. Doubtless it was used also for sealing letters.

All the protective boxes in PLATE 119 date from 1830 to 1860, the square-based box, the one with the view on it and the "spinning top" pattern being the latest. The circular open stand, with striker on base, was used from 1860 to 1900 and the ebony ash tray, with holder for safety match box, brings treen match stands up to date. Behind the "fire piston" is a Russian, nineteenth-century pocket match box of carved birch.

Believe it or not, explosive cigars did not commence as a joke. Originally like fusees, they were special matches for lighting cigars and were fitted on ends of cigars and "struck" whilst in position. Mostly they emanated from Austria and Germany between 1840 and 1845.

It is interesting that if matches were made of a quick-firing wood, they would be consumed too rapidly, so they are made chiefly from aspen or white Canadian pine, which ignite so slowly that they must be coated with paraffin wax at the head end, in order to create an inflammable vapour. Watch the wax ooze out on the next one you light.

BELLOWS—Great artists of the Renaissance in Italy and France especially, lavished their finest skill on bellows, which were carved elaborately on both sides. Two fine Italian examples, formerly in the Ledger collection, are in PLATE 121. The smaller is 28 in., the larger 33 in. long. Both are walnut, carved deeply on the faces with winged caryatid figures, scrolls, cartouches and grotesque heads, in the style of the second half of the sixteenth century. On the back of the smaller is carved a large cherub head with folded wings and on the reverse of the larger, a design formed of acanthus leaves. Both have finely chased bronze nozzles. Some English seventeenth- and eighteenth-century specimens, though less elaborate, possess artistic merit and follow furniture fashions in oak, walnut and mahogany. Usually they have long brass nozzles.

SPILL VASES—Improved standards of living in the eighteenth century and the trend for specialised articles bring us to spill vases, without which no living room was complete in Georgian and Victorian days. Of the selection in PLATE 120, the pair of "hands" (left) are probably "native" carved. Next are two Georgian urns of figured birch and walnut respectively. The two mahogany and sycamore "stickware" vases, decorated with views, date from 1850-70, and the pair of olivewood vases, with bark-ringed bases, were made about the same time. Next comes a spill vase off a Victorian smoker's table and, right, two early Tunbridge vases turned from glued up rings of various woods.

LIGHTING

From fire, we pass to light. Cave dwellers used firebrands, most ancient civilisations used oil lamps, some Pacific islanders used candlenuts. John Evelyn writes in 1670 that woods of the hornbeam, piceaster (pine) and pitch-pine were all formerly used as candles in Europe. The Middle Ages used oil lamps as well as rush-lights and soft tallow dips, which gradually developed into the hard candles used to-day.

H

The nineteenth century saw a race between improved oil lamps, gas and electricity. Colza oil lamps, introduced about 1836, were the early Victorian "party" lights, until they were superseded in 1853 by lamps burning paraffin or kerosene. Gas was discovered as an illuminant in 1795 by William Murdock, who lit his own house with it, but popular prejudice slowed its general adoption. Boulton and Paul gave the new medium a fillip by lighting their works with it in 1803 and gas street lighting, commencing in Pall Mall in 1809, soon spread to many important London streets, superseding oil lamps on standards, a few of which had been installed as early as 1684. The nineteenth century was half-way through, however, before even better class London homes had gas services extending higher than the reception rooms and in many houses, owing more to fear than cost, gas never reached the bedrooms, candles continuing as the only illuminant until electricity cheapened. It must be remembered also that early gas was not such a great improvement on candles; at first it was smelly, fed by fluctuating pressure and merely a raw, flickering flame emerging from a hole at the end of a pipe. "Batswing" and "fishtail" burners followed, but not until Welsbach, in 1885, invented the incandescent mantle did gas become a steady, white light.

Meanwhile knowledge of electricity progressed and arc lamps appeared in the eighteen fifties but, owing to large size, they were confined chiefly to street lighting and large buildings. In 1879 Sir J. Swan in England and in 1881 Thomas Edison in America did for electricity what Welsbach later did for gas by introducing incandescent electric lamps of size suitable for domestic use.

Treen for lighting consists chiefly of candlesticks, candlestands and candle boxes. None of the other media has real treen, though the preparation of both gas and electricity uses vast quantities of timber.

RUSH LIGHT NIPS—Rush lights, prepared from pith of rushes soaked in oil or fat, were used by the Romans and described by Homer 1000 B.C. Probably they never died out; certainly they were used in the Middle Ages and continued in peasant cottages until the nineteenth century ended.

English rush light nips generally have iron stems and nips and wooden bases, sometimes roughly squared, at other times simply turned. Some are floor standing models, with adjustable ratchets to raise or lower the light. Crudity of base shows poverty more certainly than antiquity. Generally, bases of eighteenth-century specimens, when turned, are steeper in profile than nineteenth-century ones. The example in PLATE 123 is quite a good eighteenth-century model, with yew wood base. The side cup, which is a part of one "leg" of the hinged rush nip is, on these later models, intended as a candle holder for special occasions, or as a douser for the rush, but on early specimens the cup is small and intended only as a douser.

CANDLESTICKS—There is nothing so rare in treen as early candlesticks of simple form. The unsuitability of the material for the purpose, except when protected by a metal cup, is obviously the reason. The candle needed only to be forgotten for a few minutes and the candlestick had gone or was so damaged that, being of little value, it was cast away. This is doubtless the reason for scarcity of old specimens, not that they were made in limited quantities. Our ancestors used wood for its cheapness, ease of working and availability and largely without regard to fitness for purpose. For example, when the hearth moved from the centre of the room, even early chimneys were wooden; the results can easily be guessed. In an endeavour to check fire risks, the Normans introduced the "couvrefeu", or curfew—a large metal dome which had to be put over the fire at "black-out" time. The time was signalled by a tolling bell and, by the thirteenth

123 Fine 18th century lacemaker's candle stand, various candlesticks, candle box and rush nip. The combined rush nip and candle holders with ejectors is unusual

124 Adjustable candle stands, candle box, double and triple twist candlesticks, etc., and a rare Georgian night-light holder and dish warmer

125 Adjustable coffee stool

126 Four 18th century mangling boards, standing distaff and handsman's stick

127 Carved wooden stirrup

century, curfew had come to mean the bell, though the couvrefeu vessel was used in some parts of Europe until the eighteenth century. Timber chimneys finally departed in 1467, when it was enacted "that no chimneys of tre be suffered but that the owners make hem of bryke or stone".

Wooden candlesticks are divided into two types: simple domestic and elaborate ecclesiastical and palace types. Wooden examples earlier than the eighteenth century have rarely survived, unless elaborate and valued as works of art. Another reason for the survival of palatial wooden examples is because they are mostly pricket types and their tops were always protected from burning by a metal grease pan.

It is dangerous to be dogmatic about dates of antique candlesticks, even when their features are outstandingly obvious. The same designs continued century after century and I have yet to meet the man who, on appearance, can tell whether a wooden piece is 300 or 400 years old.

Two fine pairs of candlesticks, of which one pair is probably sixteenth century, Italian, are illustrated in PLATE 122. The taller pair, 21 in. high, is gilt pine and consists of hexagonal columns formed with three large and three small sides, decorated with classical carved mouldings and cherub heads, whose respective outstretched wings meet. They stand on three rather flat scrolled feet and are typical of designs in wood and bronze of their period. Their condition is good, considering their probable age. The smaller pair, 19¾ in. high, of (pear?) wood, are patinated to the colour and lustre of bronze. They are late seventeenth-century design and their twisted pillars, intertwined flowers and foliage show baroque influence. Their acanthus scrolled, bell-shaped knops act as canopies for three beautifully executed cherub heads, with wings folded in the manner beloved of Grinling Gibbons. Their acanthus scroll carved feet curve gracefully. Their prickets, which appear to be original, are also wooden, so it seems probable that they were never intended for use, but were wood patterns made as a "try-out", probably for bronze.

Little seems known of simple treen candlesticks until the end of the seventeenth century. I have seen only one earlier—a German specimen of pricket type, dating from about 1500, in the Victoria and Albert Museum. By analogy with metal, we have a good idea of fifteenth-, sixteenth- and seventeenth-century wood forms and it is a popular fallacy that although the socket candleholder was introduced in the fourteenth century, it was uncommon for domestic use until at least 200 years later. This is incorrect; the Romans used socket candlesticks, which may have been lost again in the Dark Ages and not reintroduced until the fourteenth century, but paintings of domestic interiors from the mid-fifteenth century onwards, almost invariably show socket types. The pricket, especially for candles of larger diameter, has continued in churches to the present day.

In design the two tall ring-turned oak candlesticks (outside, 123) appear to be my earliest domestic examples. They are 24 in. high and their simple stems and slightly concave plain cups proclaim seventeenth century, but I doubt whether they have anything like this age. Burning of sockets and scraping off or polishing in of surplus tallow give an entirely false impress of age to candlesticks. I have no doubt that my earliest domestic specimen is the crude and simply turned elm stick in front of the lacemaker s candlestand in the same picture. Its general form, the small spread of its base, the fact that, including its base, it is all turned out of one piece, combined with its unmistakable signs of wear and the condition of the wood, point to it being not later than 1700.

The small boxwood double candlestick of about 1780 (left, 123), with three dainty spreading spindle feet, is of good quality and interesting because of the alternative rush nip in the centre, the height adjustment of the candleholders by set screw acting on stem, the brass lining to nip and candleholders and the automatic ejection of candle ends by pressing upward the knobs under the holders. The short mahogany candlestick (right), with global socket, is an unusual eighteenth-century design. The 20-in. high, walnut candlestick, formed like an inverted trumpet, with drip pan below candle socket and "cup" handle, is a type commonly found in the West Country and in Brittany, usually made of highly glazed pottery, brass or copper. It is not a practical design in wood and was probably made during the last century for ornament.

The two therm-shaped mahogany candlesticks on square base (central, 124), have brass necks and drip pans and are typical Regency pieces of about 1810–20. Next on the right, the two small ebony candlesticks are twentieth century, copying a late eighteenth-century design.

The 12½-in. high baluster turned walnut candlesticks (122) are a genuine old pair, which probably approximate to the contemporary silver design of 1794. The slender baluster and ring-turned mahogany candlestick (centre) is 7⅞ in. high and inlaid with flowers. It is Dutch, of about 1740–50.

Flat-bottomed chamber or saucer candlesticks are represented by the nineteenth-century olivewood pair (centre, 120). The other three specimens (same picture) are travelling candlesticks and are described in Part 13. Left front of PLATE 124 is a rare Georgian mahogany nightlight holder of about 1780. The sides of tambour work and the bottom are brass lined. As similar patterns occur in pottery and were used for keeping food warm, doubtless treen specimens served the same purpose.

In domestic wooden candlesticks it now only remains to discuss "twists"; there are solid twists, both of rope or "Dutch" type, as well as English double rope or "barley sugar", also the more airy "open double twists", as right of PLATE 124, and "open triple twists" as on the left. They have all enjoyed popularity ever since the seventeenth century and as open twists are regarded by turners as exhibition pieces, they will probably continue in similar form for many years yet. The dates of individual specimens are problematical. They are delicate and, even if treated carefully, break easily, so it is likely that most existing specimens were made during the last century. Mine are not new, nor are they "period". The "triples" are oak, probably about 100 years old; the "doubles", which are good quality, are walnut and probably date from 1800–10. In all modern specimens I have examined, the turners have "cheated" by removing the centre cores from inside the twists with a drill, then pelleting the holes at the end. The older ones, such as those illustrated, are "scooped" from the sides and without holes at top or bottom.

Many people exaggerate the importance of shape of candle sockets and contend, because of the prevalence of seventeenth-century "cotton reel" and straight cups in metal, that urns, vases or inverted bell-shaped cups were all eighteenth-century inventions. All these shapes occur in earlier work, particularly Italian Renaissance. The eighteenth century, apart from certain ornamental detail, was mainly a classical revival. In candlestick bases there are two distinct styles: flat bases, which seem to have originated in Western Europe and cylindrical deep bases, sometimes slightly conical, which came from the East. They chased each other in and out of fashion, the fifteenth- and early sixteenth-century popular "flat" largely giving way to the "deep" cylindrical in the late sixteenth and early seventeenth century, after which the pendulum swung again. During most of this period, however, the top of the base was the drip pan and not until the mid-seventeenth century did the drip pan separate from the base and start climbing upwards, staying halfway for some time, but reaching the underside of the cup generally between 1675 and 1700. By 1800 the pan had tended to become a separate metal or glass disc on top of the cup.

CANDLES—This brings us to candles, for the drip pan's climb was due to their gradual improvements. Whilst fine wax candles were used ecclesiastically from early days, the first advance on rush light in the ordinary home was the soft tallow "dip"— simply a wick repeatedly dipped in tallow, or other suitable fat, until it attained the required diameter. Poorer people made their own, but in the fifteenth century, if not earlier, in important towns travelling candlemakers visited larger houses and made candles for the inmates. These early candles gave a poor, flickering light and needed frequent snuffing or trimming of their crude, loosely twisted, round wicks, which, not burning as fast as the fat, tended to fall into it.

Wax candles came into use in wealthy homes in the sixteenth century, but were expensive and largely "party" elsewhere until about 1800. As late as 1794, Parson Woodforde records in his diary "Dined at Mr. Mellish yesterday. Mr. Mellish treated very handsomely indeed. Wax candles in the evening . . ." and in 1795 "To Yollop, Haberdasher, for half a dozen pound of Kensington or London Mould candles, 4 to the lb. paid him 5/–"—a great sum in those days.

Moulded candles had been introduced in the fifteenth century, but were much dearer than dips, owing to highest grade tallow being necessary, to obviate excessive shrinkage. Iron moulds were usually employed, but in the Dryfus collection in Geneva there were formerly two wooden specimens, one dated 1578, the other 1698. Hard composite candles and flat plaited wicks, designed to bend downwards into the flame and be totally consumed, were both nineteenth-century inventions. Until these came, footmen attended to snuff candles dripping from chandeliers and to trim wicks. This was no mean task; at the coronation banquet of George II, Westminster Hall was lighted by 1,800 hanging candles, in addition to those on the tables. At a function which I attended at the Goldsmiths' Hall, sometime between the two wars, their fine old hall, some 80 ft. by 40 ft., was lit by 250 candles and the light, though beautifully soft, was very subdued. With our bright, evenly-lit rooms, it is easy to forget the dim light in rooms of even a century ago, with their pools of wavering light from scattered candles.

CANDLE STANDS AND ARMS—Reflecting thus, one appreciates the necessity for the devices used to keep candles at right heights for work and recreation. In the eighteenth century furniture became very functional and provision was made in many pieces for holding candlesticks and brackets. Bureau-bookcases, music stands and architects' tables were provided with candlesticks and mirrors particularly had candle brackets, in order to reflect light as well as for toilet purposes. There were also separate adjustable candle brackets, such as the homely nineteenth-century Tunbridgeware expanding arm (119) made to screw on a mantelshelf or table. The split finial at the top of its adjustable rise-and-fall stem held a chained snuffer; the double ring below was to clip on a draught or fire shield.

Girandoles, or torchères, to stand on floors, were made in the style of each succeeding period from the Tudors and adjustable candlesticks were made in metal; but it seems to have been left to the Georgians to invent adjustable candlestands to seat on a table. These, by simple rise movements, compensated for the diminution of the candles. A mid-eighteenth-century example, in faded mahogany, is near the right of PLATE 124. Next is a rosewood specimen of about 1820, with brass inner stem; left is a late eighteenth-century walnut specimen. After about 1830 the best have "stops" on the inner stems, so that they cannot be pulled right out. For some inexplicable reason, they are often confused with wig stands.

Another device for making expensive candles serve to the utmost in cottage and workshop, was the lacemakers' candlestand, or candlestool. Specimens are now very rare. That shown (central, 123) is oak and, for this class of piece, unusually well made; it is early or mid-eighteenth century. The stem of the tripod is hollow, the candle "stick" moving up and down, controlled by a spring. The four glass flasks, called "flashes", were filled with water and the candle height adjusted so that the single illuminant would send through them four circles of light concentrated on to the lacemaking pillows of four workers grouped round the stand. This candlestand was among the pieces which I "televised" in the B.B.C. programme of August 20, 1947, the first time that treen had ever "gone on the air". A similar device, with a single flash, was used by watchmakers and other craftsmen engaged on fine work. The "flashes" in the photograph are modern reproductions; their necks should taper more, so that they go further into their holders.

CANDLEBOXES—Our last item, the candlebox, played an important part in olden times. A Normandy walnut example is central in PLATE 124 and a mahogany box, common in Georgian days, towards the left of PLATE 123. Both have sliding fronts, but with Georgian types the front sometimes became the lid, the boxes being made for horizontal use or for hanging on walls.

Double candleboxes, with two lids and two parallel compartments, one sub-divided into three smaller sections, were combined candle and tinder boxes, the three small sections being for tinder, flint and steel. Single boxes of candlebox form, but divided as described, are treen tinder boxes. The use of candleboxes is already so far forgotten that they are often described as knifeboxes. It is noteworthy that the first recorded use of mahogany in England was for a candlebox, made by a cabinetmaker named Wollaston of Long Acre, at the end of the seventeenth century.

The general place for candleboxes was the foot of the staircase leading to the bedrooms, where candlesticks were grouped on a table or ledge, ready to light you to bed. In old houses, a recess or niche in the wall at the bottom of the stairs, now occupied by ornaments, was designed for candlesticks, with one of which in hand, as Pepys has told us, "and so to bed".

*   *   *

COLLECTORS NOTES

Arranged and described so well that even adults can understand it, the history of firemaking, with the devices employed, is displayed in the "Children's Gallery" at the Science Museum, South Kensington. A large proportion of the exhibits is comprised in the unique Bryant and May Loan Collection of Firemaking Appliances. The story of lighting is told in the Museum by actual devices of the periods and by panoramas, press-button illuminated.

The ethnographical collections in the British Museum and the Pitt Rivers Museum, Oxford, include examples of native firemaking appliances from all parts of the world.

The Wallace Collection contains magnificent Italian Renaissance carved bellows.

Tinder boxes, sulphur matches, rush light holders and candle moulds are in museums throughout the country, but include little treen. A section in Somerset County Museum, Taunton, is devoted to lighting

I know of no comprehensive collection of wooden candlesticks, but Luton Museum has an unusually large selection of nineteenth-century and a few eighteenth-century specimens. The Victoria and Albert Museum possesses fire bellows, and a beautiful pair of carved pearwood domestic candlesticks of about 1700, in the style of Cesar Bagard of Nancy, France. Lacemakers' candlestands are in the Bucks County Museum, Aylesbury, and the Rev. C. J. Sharp's Museum, Shepreth.

128 Icelandic porringers

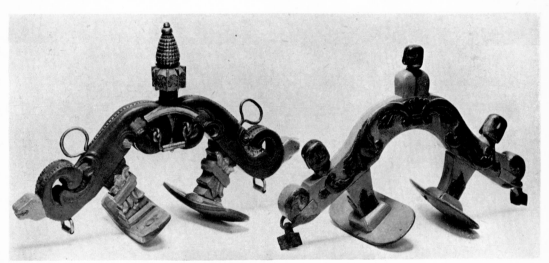

129 Norwegian horse neck saddles

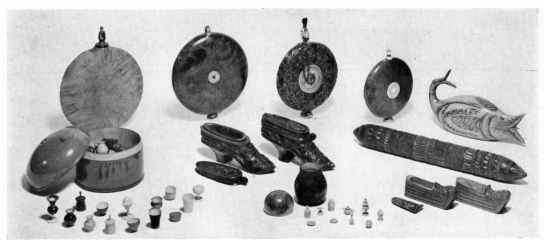

130 Scandinavian snuff flasks, shoe snuff boxes and pencil box. Russian miniature turned toys

131   Carved washing bats

132   Scandinavian drinking vessels

PART SIXTEEN

THE TREEN OF NORTH-WEST EUROPE

WELL forested countries, lacking many other raw materials, can enjoy a high standard of comfort and prosperity. In Norway, Sweden, Finland, Latvia, Estonia and parts of Russia, wood is the universal provider and the economy of these countries has been built largely on exports of timber and wood products. Men and women in these countries are born in the tradition of wood craftsmanship, for timber supplies the building material of the majority and most of the domestic articles in use, as well as the fuel. On the coasts, fishing and merchandise-carrying boats, largely of timber are primarily the means of living, while inland, forestry, plymaking, cooperage, match manufacture, turnery and general woodwork employ large percentages of the populations.

The vast forests of these northern climes consist mainly of pine, birch, beech and alder, which provide more useful than beautifully grained timbers. Consequently, bold carving and vividly coloured paints are introduced extensively, to make useful articles beautiful. Fitness for purpose is rarely sacrificed to ornament, but ordinary domestic articles are invariably attractive.

Too often the treen of all these countries, as well as that of Denmark, Holland and North Germany, is classified as Scandinavian, or even more restrictedly as Norwegian. The style and ornament of woodwork employed in the Scandinavian Peninsula and round the Baltic shores, as well as in North-West Russia and Iceland, possess considerable similarity and, without definite knowledge of place of origin, it is often impossible to say from which country an article emanates. Traditional patterns being passed from father to son, make accurate dating equally difficult.

The Educational Museum, Haslemere, Surrey, is an excellent place for learning to identify, as far as possible, North-West European treen. The Museum's comprehensive exhibit of "Peasant Arts" was mostly collected personally by the Rev. Gerald S. Davies in North-West Europe. Some specimens date back to the sixteenth century.

Whilst the peasants of nearly all the countries described use colour and decorate their woodwork with geometrical chip carving, acanthus scrolls, rope mouldings and figures of lions, horses, dragons and dogs, nearly all examples possess some characteristics which help identification. Norway and Sweden particularly seem to have adopted curved and carved outlines and relief carving, with an emphasis on bold sweeps, scrolls, lettering and monograms. These features show in the horse saddles (129), the Norwegian handsman's stick (126), the cake box (137) and the two mangling boards (left, 126). A common feature of Norwegian carving is the very square human head, appearing on one of the horse saddles. North Germany favours human figures and often ornament is distinctly Gothic. Generally, Swedish treen resembles Norwegian and where painted, red, blue, green and yellow are popular combinations, but the Swedes have also developed a distinctive and finely-carved fluted pattern of the type familiar on Sheffield plate. The flutes may be straight and vertical, or spiralling, as in the double drinking cup (135). The wood selected is usually birch, carefully selected for burr figure and the flutes are ornamented with bone studs.

Holland, lacking much wood, tends to flat designs with the obvious desire to economise material. The ornament consists almost invariably of intricate small scale geometrical designs, covering the whole surface, the carved roundel being prominent, as in the Friesland footwarmer (133) and the two mangling boards from the same province (right, 126). Dutch taste is usually considered more sombre than that of the other north-western countries. This impression prevails because dark brown or black oak is particularly favoured, without decoration in colour. Treen must be considered, however, against its intended background. In Scandinavia, wood is the traditional house building material inside and out; with a background of wood, in large part unpainted, the bright colours of treen provide a much needed contrast. Holland, however, has used brick construction for centuries and with interior walls plastered and whitened and often a floor of red quarry tiles, the sombre treen, intermingled with brass, copper and pewter, forms an effective contrast.

Individual Danish treen sometimes shows all the features already described but *en masse* has the distinctive character of daintiness. Much of the seventeenth to nineteenth-century Danish treen, like the furniture, wall panelling and ceiling beams, is simple, sparse in carving and relying on painted ornament. The favourite decorative subjects are vases and urns of rather formally arranged but natural flowers, wreaths and sprays, all in charming colours and generally against a blue background. Occasionally, scenic panels and figures are introduced; painted dates, initials and love tokens are common. Whilst the carving is probably no finer than that of other North-West European countries, a lighter feeling is introduced by piercing wherever possible, without reducing the tracery below the minimum section necessary for strength. Daintily turned and fretted balusters are introduced wherever continuous surfaces are unnecessary.

An interesting piece of Danish treen is the "kaffestol" or coffee stool (125). It is arranged so that the stool seat, pivoted in front, can be raised at the back by a winch and cord, thus ensuring coffee emerging free from grounds. The specimen comes from the island of Amager.

Iceland is the greatest puzzle. The island has neither metal nor trees. The main supply of wood, until recently, was driftwood and wreckage. The craving to make and beautify has had, therefore, to compete with the natural instinct to husband every available spar for winter fuel, yet so far has love of beauty triumphed, that Iceland has contributed some of the most satisfying and restrained designs and delicate execution. Geometrical patterns, leaving sufficient plain surface as contrast, as in the porringers dated 1875 (128), are fairly common, but fine, free scrolls, dragons, horses and runic lettering are other characteristics. Probably the exceptional value of timber to the Icelander has contributed in ensuring the care everywhere evident, that design and craftsmanship shall be worthy.

Russia is so vast that its treen is naturally most varied. In the East it is Oriental, in the West, European. Of the European, that from the latitudes between those of Holland and Iceland follows closely the shapes and ornament of its western neighbours The carved designs are largely geometrical, with the roundel predominating; often the infilling of the roundel is some variant of a rose design. Plants are largely portrayed, rather crudely and with sparse detail, but generally more naturalistically and less formally than in Scandinavia. Typical Russian motifs are the "Sirin" and the "Alconost", the "Swastika" and figures with raised arms and outstretched hands. The "Sirin" and "Alconost" were mythological birds, which had power to assume the shapes of women and they were usually depicted with face, arms and upper part of the body of a woman and the lower part of the body, legs, claws, wings and tail of a bird. The "swastika" or "Flyfot" was symbolic of good luck in Russia, as in Greece and India, from earliest times. Figures with raised and outstretched arms simply signify adoration. Another common motif consists of symbolic animals such as lions, horses, stags or birds facing each other and separated by the tree of life.

In Russian the word "krasny" denotes "red" or "beautiful" and where colours are used, red is usually predominant, with a fair sprinkling of brown, blue and white. In Lithuania the colours second in popularity to red, are green and yellow.

133   Russian shoe cleaning box and Friesland foot warmer, intricately chip carved

134   18th and 19th century carved tankards, dippers, tumbler holder and spoon

135   Swedish double drinking cup.   Rare coffee grinder hollowed from a burry walnut root
and dated 1706 and Norwegian coffee pot

136 Norwegian butter mould, salt boxes, and Russian bread plate

137 Butter mould closed. Early 19th century cake box and engraved ladle

Availability of timber varies considerably among north-west European countries, but certain common factors have combined to create their virile peasant woodcraft and have caused what initially appears incomprehensible expenditure of labour on simple, everyday articles. All these countries have long, cold, dark winters. All have or had small scattered communities, entirely self dependent for their needs and pastimes. Finally, they all had the peasant custom of making love tokens, more fully described in Part 4. These factors combined, account for the labour expended on woodcraft, "wood-sloyd" or "husflid". "Sloyd" is an English word derived from the Swedish "SLÖJD". It signifies the home manufacture of articles by individuals or families, as opposed to factory mass production. "Husflid" is the Norwegian term for "home industry". Both apply particularly to the work of the peasant, who was and still largely is carpenter, joiner, carver, turner and painter by turn, during the long winter, when there is little that he can do out of doors and while the women sit at their looms, spinning wheels or lace bobbins. With many months compulsorily spent indoors, time is often of less account than material and consequently each man necessarily develops the patience to create for home, carriage gear or sledge, a wealth of beautiful objects in accordance with his taste and skill.

MANGLING BOARDS—From general similarities and local variations in design we pass to specific articles of domestic woodware. They cover both the familiar range of English treen and some additional articles.

An instance is the ornamental mangling board or calender, sometimes incorrectly called an ironing board and usually described, sometimes wrongly, as Norwegian. Used in conjunction with a rolling pin, like a pastry roller, the two implements combined were the forerunner of modern mangles. The wet clothes were wound round the roller, which was then run backwards and forwards by pressure on the heavy board, arranged at right angles on top of the roller; the right hand gripped the handle of the board and the left pressed on its opposite end. The mangling roller and a "bat" were used formerly in England and the two appliances are shown together in PLATE 115.

Norwegian mangling boards usually have the rolling surface somewhat upward curved at each end and tapering in width. Both these features occur in the two boards (left, 126); the extreme left example, with handle formed as a cannon, is of birch, painted red and green, a popular Scandinavian colour combination of the eighteenth and nineteenth centuries. It is $\frac{3}{4}$ in. thick, 27 in. long, 3 in. wide at handle end, tapering to $2\frac{1}{2}$ in. Usually these boards taper the opposite way. In addition to scrolls carved in relief and chip carved bands, it is carved with initials and the date 1833. It is lighter and more delicately carved than most Norwegian boards. The heavier board, with horse handle, is eighteenth-century work of birch and much more typical, being $1\frac{1}{2}$ in. thick and narrower at the handle than the other end. It measures $28\frac{3}{4}$ in. by $3\frac{1}{2}$ in. at the handle and $4\frac{1}{2}$ in. at the other end.

The two boards (right, 126) are typical eighteenth-century Friesland examples; they weigh much less than the Norwegian, because of the need for timber economy. The longer, though 34 in. by $5\frac{3}{4}$ in., is only $\frac{1}{2}$ in. thick, whilst the smaller, which measures $33\frac{1}{2}$ in. by $4\frac{7}{8}$ in., is only $\frac{3}{8}$ in. thick. The larger is black, the smaller dark brown oak. The latter, in addition to chip carved roundels, also bears a carved inscription saying that Gysbert Cornelis son of E. Cornelis washes white and mangles well, etc.

These Friesland mangling boards, unlike Scandinavian ones, have no handles, do not taper and are flat and thin. These differences seem to have confused the late Owen Evan-Thomas who, in *Domestic Utensils of Wood*, illustrates a French and Friesland mangling board of this type, described under the heading of wooden tallies. Actually, the photograph of the "Dutch tally" in his book shows clearly that it bears an inscription somewhat similar to that on one of my boards, stating that it is for washing and mangling. I do not wish to infer by this that tally boards of the type described do not exist. I think that they do and that they were used for reckoning in public houses as well as for orders for tradesmen. Their purpose would lead one to expect them to be wider than mangling boards, although in general outline they may resemble the Friesland variety. I have met several of the latter in antique shops, described as tally boards, but this may be due to Evan-Thomas' description.

The earliest mangling board which I have is a French specimen, carved with fleur-de-lys and dated 1649.

WASHING BATS—Although washing bats, called alternatively beaters, beetles or batlets, are found elsewhere than North-West Europe, it is doubtful whether anywhere else are they so decorative. In PLATE 131, left to right, the first three are Norwegian and in 1 and 3 the familiar heart denotes a love token. The fourth is Russian and that on the extreme right, the only one not painted in bright colour, is Dutch. These examples vary in length from 13 to 20 in.

DISTAFFS—The specimen illustrated in PLATE 126 is Scandinavian and its graceful stem is attractively coloured in faded reds, greens and blues. The "comb" and the collar, down to the square above the rope moulding, revolves on a pivot and one of its rings is carved with seven hearts, showing that this was a love token. Another ring carries the initials "AML". The height is $42\frac{1}{2}$ in. Note how the "corn-stook" carving near the top resembles that on the cylindrical pencil box (130).

In addition to standing distaffs, all the north-west European countries used hand models and other spinning wheel attachments in a wide variety of attractively carved and fretted designs.

FOOT WARMERS—These are used throughout North-West Europe, particularly in Friesland. They are usually of oak, stained black and with a solid base, as shown on the right of PLATE 133. The hinged door in front and the other side and top panels have finely carved and pierced roundels. Like most Friesland treen, all surfaces are carved, including the base. These boxes were fitted with earthenware or iron pans for charcoal and were used as combined footstools and footwarmers in churches. The example illustrated is seventeenth or early eighteenth century and shows extensive marks of burning inside the top. It is 8 in. high and 9 in. by 8 in. on plan. The name "Maria Weser" is carved on the edge of the door.

BOXES—Carved wood boxes were formerly and in many places still are used for bread, cakes, butter, cheese, tea, games, knitting needles and divers other purposes. Unless of almost "trunk" size, they mostly differ fundamentally from their English counterparts in the absence of corner joints; actually corners are usually non-existent, but where they occur, they are pegged or strengthened with metal bands. The smaller boxes generally were made either like the early eighteenth-century Scandinavian salt box (right, 136), which is hollowed from a solid block of oak, or else they were constructed from beech or pine, steamed, bent and laced with fibre to the desired shape. Examples are the oval salt or butter box (136) and the $11\frac{1}{2}$ in. diameter cake or bread box (right, 137), both of which are Scandinavian. The latter is spiritedly carved with flowers and scrolls and gaily painted in blue and brown. Its carving tells that John Hansen made it on April 3, 1822. If he completed it that single day he was a fast worker. As is customary in this form of construction, the wood is only $\frac{1}{8}$ in. thick, with the rim edges pegged to the top and bottom, without nails or screws.

The early twentieth-century Russian two-compartment shoe-cleaning box (left, 133), with rounded angles and central carrying handle, is practical and pleasing. The chipped ornament is painted scarlet and green, on a flesh-coloured background.

HORSE HARNESS—Scandinavian harness saddles, stirrups and horse collars are most decorative. The two early nineteenth-century harness saddles (129) are carved and painted and are a simple type, many being pierced elaborately in addition to being carved. These saddles fit the necks of the horses. In the example on the left, the reins pass through the rings on the saddle, while in the other they pass over the carved heads. The metal loops hanging below originally had bells suspended from them.

Carved stirrups like PLATE 127 were made of wood on account of its abundant availability, because of its good insulation against cold and because of the ease with which it could be formed into a toe muff.

Old horse collars followed the form of English ones, but were carved elaborately and painted *en suite* with the last two items.

VESSELS CARVED FROM THE SOLID—The finest coffee or spice grinder I have ever seen is the specimen, probably Dutch, central in PLATE 135. It is not cabinet made, but has been hollowed from a single block, a burry walnut root, which has been carved and hand moulded. It was made in 1706 and the photograph, taken from the back, show that date and the initials "J.B." on one of the raised panels between the pilasters of the plinth. The steel base-tray, bun feet and ribbed steel band to which the lid is hinged are hand wrought. The handle is detachable. The berries or spices, fed in at the top, when ground fell into the drawer in the base, which pulls out from the side opposite to that illustrated.

Some typical Scandinavian vessels, carved from the solid, are shown at the bottom of PLATE 134. These include two painted dipper vessels of traditional form, a Scandinavian spoon and a tumbler holder, both pierced and carved with acanthus scrolls, and a small eighteenth-century tankard. On the shelf are four tankards carved from the solid, with handles pegged on. On the left is an elaborately carved Norwegian tankard 10½ in. high, 6½ in. in diameter. Next is a superb quality Norwegian tankard, 10 in. high, 6¼ in. in diameter. The body of the vessel is unusually finely carved with a wide band of intertwined flowering branches, between borders of leaves and conventional carved mouldings. The cover is carved similarly and surmounted by a carved and pierced dome and whorl finial. The handle is carved with foliage and a leaf scroll thumb piece. The two tankards on the right are birch and with relief carved lions on the lids, lions forming thumb lifts and grotesque animals as feet, are typical of these well-known north-west European drinking vessels of the late eighteenth and early nineteenth centuries. The taller of the two is dated 1809.

The enormous drinking vessel (centre, 132), with bowl carved from a single block 8¼ in. high and 8¾ in. across, is a late nineteenth-century copy of a Swedish horned "kasa" or beaker, of a type mentioned in Claus Magnus' work on the Scandinavian Peoples (1555). Commencing in the Middle Ages as beakers from the same common stock as Scottish "bickers" (32), these Scandinavian versions gradually developed horns, which eventually were linked into handles by pierced and engraved scrollwork. The specimen illustrated is 29½ in. high overall and 22 in. across the horns. Its background is painted red, except the rims of the bowl and the two horns, which expose the unpainted birch. It is decorated overall with natural coloured flowers, leaves and scrolls and black incised lines. Inside the bowl is an inscription which translated reads "Merry Guest drinks best". On the exterior is part of the Swedish Coat of Arms.

Although the peasants of Northern and North-Western Europe seem to have been generally abstemious, it was their custom at certain festivals to indulge in drinking bouts and it was considered quite praiseworthy to get drunk and see who could empty one of these tremendous ale bowls with the fewest draughts. Horned "kasas" were designed to allow room for the drinker's head between the bowl rim and the underside of the scrolled handle. When drinking, the handle gradually passed over the drinker's head, forming a wreath and finally resting against the back of his neck as he drained the last dregs.

Large drinking bowls, carved from the solid with two outward scrolling handles terminating in crude carved horse heads, have been used for many centuries throughout Scandinavia. Most old ones still extant bear dates of the last quarter of the eighteenth century. That right of PLATE 132 is dated 1787.

PLATE 135, left, is the Swedish double cup carved from birch root and ornamented with spiral fluting and bone studs, to which reference has been made already. The eighteenth century Norwegian coffee pot (right) is an example of good but simple form and virile low relief carving. On the body of the pot a hunter is depicted, shooting a boar which in turn is pursued by a bear. The neck of the pot bears an inscription. On the lid, in a circular lozenge, is a relief of a lion and the "lift" of the lid is formed by a seated animal. The pot is hollowed from birch root, with the spout inserted and the handle pegged on. The overall height is 9 in. and diameter $7\frac{1}{2}$ in.

Wooden bowls of every size are common and, unless carved, are indistinguishable from their English counterparts. A well carved Russian bread plate, formerly owned by Princess Beatrice, is in PLATE 136. Some characteristically ornamented spoons and ladles from North-West Europe are illustrated in PLATE 44, and a Russian flower vase and a Norwegian two-handled drinking bowl in PLATE 79.

COOPERED VESSELS—Vessels built up with staves held by bandings of willow, ash, beech or cane were and are used much more in North and North-West Europe than in England. In this type of construction there also occurs a two-horned "kasa" or straight-sided beaker. The horns have an outward spread to form handles and the whole vessel is near akin to the Scottish "bicker". The main difference is that in the Swedish or Norwegian version the staves are all made from one variety of wood and the carved handles usually represent an animal head, or less often a complete animal, as in the fine lion handled "kasa" (left, 132). Vessels of this type date from the late seventeenth or early eighteenth century and were still used in the nineteenth. The specimen pictured is 5 in. deep and 8 in. across the bowl.

Drinking tankards are often made in this construction and the same form is used largely for purposes other than drinking. The Iceland porringers, carved with the date 1875 (128), are an example. More unusual is the butter mould (left, 136, and left, 137), with the impress design in the lid. Its height is 11 in., diameter 5 in. and depth inside the crown of lid $5\frac{1}{2}$ in. Cane-bound coopered jugs for various liquids and coffee pots were other commonplaces and are still in use outside the cities. Tubs, kegs and barrels, unless carved, mostly resemble our own.

SNUFF TREEN—Scandinavian pocket snuff boxes in the eighteenth century developed in an attractive circular flask form (130). Usually they are made from carefully selected birch or maple burrs or roots, with bone or silver nozzles and filling caps, sometimes with a turned bone or silver "boss" in the centre. The filling cap unscrews and the snuff was introduced from a spouted rasp. In the nineteenth century snuff boxes in the form of shoes and sabots became popular all over Europe and some finely carved ones are in the same plate, together with a curious table type of snuff box with fish and bird terminals.

TOYS—Gay colours and individuality are nowhere more outstanding than in the delightful carved toys of North-West Europe and doubtless the children's pleasure has at least been equalled by the joy of creating the quaint jointed animals and puppets, tumbling and climbing figures and miniature furniture and utensils. Lack of space unfortunately forbids a representative selection, but PLATE 130 shows two boxes of miniature turned Russian toys. The larger box and its contents are of birch, brightly enamelled in reds, blues, gold and violet. The turnings, of paper thickness, vary in height from ½ in. to 1 in. The smaller box and its toys are uncoloured.

If noise and happiness are synonymous and judging by the radio they are to many, then childhood in the traditional Russian peasant home must have been very happy, for there the grotesque human dolls, horsemen and animals were generally fitted with whistles and the toys were called "SVYSTUNI"—that is, "whistles".

*   *   *

COLLECTORS NOTES

In addition to the items pictured in this chapter, collectors will find plenty of other interesting treen from North-West Europe, such as plates with carved and painted rims, decorated bowls, spice boxes, gingerbread and cake moulds, quaint four-sided candlesticks and stands, combined calendar and watchstands, measuring sticks, bellows, hand mirror cases, spinning wheels, shuttles, bobbins and hand distaffs, the latter being particularly decorative. There is also a large range of purpose made carved boxes, fitted for various games, as well as for knitting needles and food storage. Circular boxes, similar to the cake-box (137), but only about 7 in. in diameter, were for " flatbrod" or oatcake. Other decorative wooden objects are carved wooden scutching or swingling knives, used for separating the flax from the boon, carved wooden doorstops encasing bricks, carved oars, ox yokes, horse collars, carved parts of sledges, carts and carriages. Old woodworkers' hand tools were also carved with individuality and skill.

Many of the items mentioned are in the Haslemere Educational Museum of Peasant Art, which also has a representative collection of tankards, beer cans, boxes, mangle boards, dairy utensils, wooden locks and a few toys, as well as contemporary peasant furniture, etc. I know of no other comprehensive collection in this country, but many of our museums, particularly the Victoria and Albert Museum, have good specimens.

Readers interested in peasant art, who have the opportunity of travelling abroad, should not fail to see the fine collections at:

DENMARK	..	Nationalmuseet, Copenhagen.
		Vendsyssels Historiake Museum, Hjorring.
		Herning Museum, Herning.
		Museet for Koldinghus Len, Kolding.
		Fyns Stiftsmuseum, Odense.
		Lolland-Falsters Stiftsmuseum, Maribo.
HOLLAND	..	The Netherlands Open Air Museum, Arnhem.
ICELAND	..	Archælogical Museum of Iceland (Thjoo), Minjasafn Islands.
NORWAY	..	Kunstindustrimuseet, Oslo.
		Stavanger Museum, Stavanger.
		Bergen Museum, Bergen.
		Vestlandske Kunstindustrimuseum, Bergen.
		Nordenfjeldske Kunstindustrimuseu, Trondheim.
		Tromsö Museum, Tromsö.
RUSSIA	..	Leontevsky Persulok (Museum of Handycrafts), Moscow.
		Zagorsk (The Toy Institute), Moscow Region.
		The Abramtsevo Estate, Moscow Region.
SWEDEN	..	Nordiska Museet, Stockholm.
		Skansen (open-air) Museet, Stockholm.
		Kulturhistoriska Museet, Lund.

In most of these places treen is displayed against the original interior background for which it was designed.

PART SEVENTEEN

THE CARE OF TREEN

"If ancient buildings nod, and threat to fall,
To patch their flaws and buttress up the wall,
Thus far 'tis duty, but here fix the mark,
For all beyond it is to touch the ark."—DRYDEN.

THE same applies to treen; too zealous restoration and repair destroys value and interest as surely as does neglect. I am often asked where repair ends and restoration begins. It is difficult to specify, but I consider repair should preserve the object and arrest further deterioration but not counteract legitimate signs of wear and tear. Some repairs and reconditioning are often necessary to preserve treen for future ages. Where new wood must be inserted, because of decay or damage, by all means stain it to match the old; do not create an eyesore, but do not disguise by faking "wear". Careful repair must be expected in an old piece and does not affect its value. If objects have had carving knocked off, I often leave it off UNLESS the missing piece creates a weakness, which will result in further damage; but in such cases I prefer to insert plain wood if I cannot carve the replacement equal to the original.

Some collectors are magpies, captivated by each new glittering find, confident that they have rescued it from oblivion, but actually consigning it to decay by starving, over heating, damp or beetle attack.

If treen is bought in good condition, all that is necessary is to maintain it. This is easy, but if its condition is bad, all or any of the following operations may be entailed: cleaning, stripping, anti-beetle treatment, repair.

CLEANING—Too many people think that dirt is the natural cover of an antique and that nothing is old unless black. This theory has no merit and sometimes black merits suspicion, being designedly a cloak for the spurious.

Treen, until clean and well polished, never looks its best. Light surface dirt can be removed with any good cleaning-wax-polish. For smooth surfaces, use a soft cloth for application and for carved surfaces a tooth brush, unless the carving is deep, intricate or delicate, when a varnish brush may be safer. Polish off with soft cloths, finishing with silk. Neglected and hungry pieces may require several applications before regaining their full beauty.

Some cases need something more drastic than wax for cleaning and, where practicable, soap and water is the obvious, quick answer. It is perfectly safe treatment for items which were made to be washed, such as eating, drinking, cooking and dairy treen, PROVIDED THAT SINCE THEIR ACTIVE DAYS HAVE ENDED, THEY HAVE NOT BEEN REPAIRED WITH ANIMAL GLUE. It is not safe to immerse anything which has had any of the old glues used in construction, for veneering or inlay, or for repair. Hot water softens wood and all treen, after immersion, should be rinsed in cold water, dried carefully and not subjected to much heat immediately; impatience to view one's latest find in all its beauty is understandable, but usually fatal. Overheating is sometimes adopted to accelerate drying and so quickly reach the waxing and polishing stage; this invariably results in splitting, warping and irreparable damage. Many pieces which cannot be safely immersed can still be cleaned, wholly or partially, by means of damp, soapy cloths.

Surface dirt which will not yield to soap and water will sometimes disappear easily when rubbed with a cloth damped by a mixture consisting of equal portions of vinegar and water, or alternatively paraffin and soapy water. Paraffin and soapy water are best used from a bottle, as they are immiscible and must be shaken frequently.

STRIPPING—There is little to choose between the vandalism which paints over polished woodwork and that which strips fine old contemporary paint, in order to apply the latest fashionable finish. I do not refer to normal repainting of old, plain surfaces in whatever colour may be fashionable, but to the stripping of polychrome or gilt from carvings, usually of pine, and their conversion into fake "limed oak".

Nevertheless, removal of dirt sometimes shows that other operations are necessary before waxing. Your purchase may have received the misguided attention of some "beautifier", who has provided an unsuitable painted or varnished surface, perhaps embellished with brush hairs and encrusted grit. In fact, like some described in this book, it may have had so many coats of paint that what was once either a smooth or a sharply carved surface, has become an undulating crust. If a stripper is required, there are several excellent proprietary brands on the market, which will remove paint or varnish without damaging finger nails or skin, as caustic soda does when used in sufficient strength to remove old paint.

Proprietary strippers are applied with a brush, left for a time to soften the paint or varnish and wiped off with a cloth or a solution of weak soda water. Repeated applications may be necessary when paint or varnish is old or thickly coated. After completing stripping and before drying and waxing, it is advisable to wash the surface with methylated spirit or other solvent advocated by the maker of the stripper and leave to dry.

Modern strippers are quick and do not soften the wood nearly as badly as caustic soda. Nevertheless, they may be found rather drastic for delicate, intricate carvings, which have become fragile with age. Such pieces I strip with acetone or carbon tetrachloride which, though more laborious, are extremely effective. The latter is only safe on light woods, because it causes fading of some of the deeper coloured varieties. The procedure is the same for either: pour out a small quantity of the liquid, dip a tooth brush or paint brush in it and brush the carving until the coating begins to dissolve, then wipe with a cloth. Repeat until the desired effect is attained. With carbon tetrachloride, speed is essential; it is extremely volatile and unless wiping follows rapidly after application, it will evaporate, leaving the coating redeposited on the surface. Only a small area, therefore, should be treated at one time. Caution is necessary when using either acetone or carbon tetrachloride; the former is inflammable and dangerous near a naked flame; the latter is non-inflammable, but has mild anæsthetic properties and should not be inhaled or used in a confined space.

REPAIR—Old treen is rarely found in mint condition. When designed correctly, its first purpose was use and its purpose and age must be considered when assessing whether its condition is good or bad. It is reasonable to expect to find some Tunbridgeware in practically mint condition: some was made less than a century ago and generally only for light and careful usage. Some fine drinking vessels of considerable antiquity are in very good condition, because they were always valuable and carefully used, in some instances only for ceremonial occasions. Conversely, kitchen, direct eating treen and other wooden objects subjected to daily use must necessarily show their honourable scars of service and I think the signs of wear and the repairs effected to keep them serviceable add additional charm and interest and are marks of esteem.

Sometimes, before executing a new repair, an old one which has been executed badly must be broken down. If it be merely a glued joint, immersion in hot water will soon open it and careful scraping with a sharp chisel or knife will remove any glue remaining. After drying, subsequent operations are similar whether the break is old or new: namely, apply glue at the temperature and in the consistency recommended by the manufacturer, bring the two broken surfaces together tightly, squeeze out the surplus glue and leave under pressure for the time stated by the maker of the adhesive. It is advisable to remove surplus glue *after* it has jellied, but *before* it has hardened completely.

Difficulty is sometimes experienced in applying the light pressure necessary while the glue is setting. If the shape of the object under repair permits, string tied tightly is simple and effective. Insertion of a match or two will adjust tension. Wads of paper or other protective material should be used on corners or sharp edges, to prevent the string marking.

Sometimes the nature of the break, particularly on small objects, makes temporary holding and positioning of fractured parts difficult while the glue is setting. I use one of the following alternatives: (a) a splint made of matches, or larger strips of wood if necessary, bound with string, or (b) gummed tape bound directly round the fracture. For temporary positioning of small projecting parts of fractured carvings, plasticine is invaluable for providing plastic and easily removable support.

So far I have only described simple repairs and I propose to go no further. If you have the experience and skill to carry out a major repair, you need no advice; without these qualifications you will be well advised to pay a competent craftsman, otherwise you will only ruin the value of your treen. Repairs involving insertion of new wood require considerable skill in matching of species and grain, in fitting and polishing. Two "don'ts": never try and bring two broken edges together if a piece between them is missing, or if, as often occurs in a bowl or cylinder, the crack occurs through stresses set up by uneven shrinkage and warping. In such cases wood inserts must be used, otherwise pressure entailed in closing one crack will induce one or more fresh ones. Secondly, never use plastic woods for replacement of missing parts; these materials have legitimate uses, such as stopping pin holes, but not for general treen repairs.

ANTI-BEETLE TREATMENT—The so-called wood worm is the grub or larvæ of a beetle. Many varieties of these beetles exist, but they constitute two main groups: those which attack standing timber and those which eat the converted, seasoned wood. Only the latter concern treen collectors and the borers responsible for most "worm holes" in old woodwork are the anobiids, commonly called furniture beetles. The full-grown larvæ are only $\frac{1}{10}$ in. to $\frac{1}{3}$ in. long, brown and of cylindrical form. One of the greatest troubles with the pest is the time which must elapse before there is any certainty of eradication. The life cycle from egg to beetle, usually about a year, sometimes takes as long as three. It is during the summer months that the beetles emerge and what is not generally known is that they then fly quite considerable distances. A good "neighbour policy" is, therefore, essential. An infested house menaces a whole neighbourhood. After mating, the beetles return and lay their eggs in cracks and crevices in the wood. Signs of recent infection are newness of holes and little piles of fine dust which surround them or which discharge on tapping the suspect object.

A number of effective proprietary insecticides are marketed, all with similar purpose—namely, to poison the wood as food for the grubs and so kill them. Some proprietary brands have the advantage of tending to preserve wood and of not destroying french polish. Where articles are only wax polished, an effective and inexpensive treatment is paraffin or turpentine, well brushed into the wood or, better still, injected with a fountain-pen filler or hypodermic syringe. For those objects which can be safely soaked, total immersion is undoubtedly best, particularly if the wood is thick. The most effective time for treatment is between March and September, when larvæ are near the surface